A Bother of Bassets

A Bother of Bassets

A History of the Working Basset

Dr Brian Wilson

DENNY PUBLISHING

First published in the UK in 2004
by Denny Publishing,

British Library Cataloguing-in-Publication Data
A catalogue record for this book
is available from the British Library

ISBN 1 903680 07 7

Typeset by Phoenix Typesetting, Auldgirth, Dumfriesshire

Production Management by Rob Dixon, Asterley, Shropshire

Printed in England by MPG Books, Bodmin, Cornwall

DENNY PUBLISHING
A division of The Richard Denny Group

01608 812424
website: www.dennypublishing.co.uk
email: publishing@denny.co.uk
8 Cotswold Business Village
Moreton-in-Marsh
Gloucestershire GL56 0JQ

Contents

Illustration Acknowledgements

p 13: Foullloux, J du. 1573 *La Vénerie*. Paris: Galiuot du Pré.
pp 15, 79, 83, 86, 88, 91, 95, 98: Private collection, Mr Brian Wilson
pp 16, 17, 19, 26, 110, 113, 123, 124: Leblanc, E. & Miller, J.A. 1987. Les Bassets Courants. Paris: Gerfaut Club.
p 20: Miss M. M. Keevil, 1997. Private papers.
p 21, 22, 81, 90, 99, 102: *Hounds*. Shrewsbury: Ravensworld.
pp 36, 67 top, 70: Private collection, Mr James Williams.
p 54: Nixon, M. R. 1999 *The Basset Hound*. Waterlooville: Kingdom Books.
p 55, 67 bottom: Appleton, D H. 1960 *The Basset Hound Handbook*. London: Nicholson & Watson.
p 59: Private collection, Mr. David Hindle.
p 68: Bryden, H. A. 1927. *Horn and Hound*. London: Methuen.
p 94: Private collection, Mr. G. Browne.
p 97: Private collection, Mr. Rory Dicker.
p 100: Private collection, Mr. Mark Guy.
pp 127, 128: Smith, A. C. 1909. *Everyman's Book of the Dog*. London: Hodder and Stoughton.

Foreword

The Onslows have been associated with the countryside for as long as I can trace them. We have all been keenly interested in country sports and animals. Our venture into keeping and hunting bassets was short, but historical. In 1872 my great grandfather, the 4th Earl of Onslow, bought the bassets which Lord Galway had imported from France. Rather than using them to flush game, he decided to use them to hunt hare as a pack, probably the first time that this had been attempted in England. This was mainly at Clandon Park in Surrey where I still live. He also showed them extensively, including at the first Cruft's Show. Not only did he import more from France, but he also bred bassets and involved himself in the breed improvements initiated by Sir Everett Millais. This all ceased when he took up his appointment as Governor General of New Zealand in 1888.

From this small start, bassets have become and still are popular, both as working hounds and as pets. My great grandfather was a founder of the Basset Hound Club and of the Masters of Basset Hounds Association, both of which still flourish. Whilst books have been written on the basset as a pet, none have ever covered, in detail, their original use as hunting hounds. I am delighted that this has now been rectified, especially as it has been done in the context of social history and of scientific research. I hope that this book gives pleasure to many and encourages all to keep field sports alive in this country.

The Earl of Onslow
Temple Court, Clandon Park, Guildford

23 August 2004

Chapter One

Introduction

THE basset has been used in the British Isles in packs for hunting hare from about 1872. Yet most books featuring bassets have been written mainly from the perspective of 'pure' bred, show hounds with, at most, a short chapter or section on hunting. Furthermore, most English books feature only one type, the smooth coated Basset Hound.

This book is written from the perspective of hunting and celebrates over forty years of hunting with bassets enjoyed by the author. Whilst recognising the so called 'pure' breeds of bassets, the book treats bassets as a group within the hound family, not as one or more specific breeds, and as a group that is dynamic and still developing. It traces how the basset has evolved in the contexts of both the social influences that have shaped the developments of dogs and hunting and in the context of the general evolution of the dog from the wolf. It looks at what distinguishes a basset from other types of hound in terms of genetics, physiology and hunting style. As every book is never totally objective and must, to some extent, reflect the background of the author, Chapter 2 gives the author's personal views and experiences of hunting hares, especially with bassets.

Every book is dependent upon the work and help of others. The bibliography is a tribute to the many whose knowledge and researches have been drawn upon and whom are hereby acknowledged. But special thanks are owed to many individuals who related their personal experiences, often loaning or giving unique written and photographic records. The book is particularly indebted to the late Miss M.M. (Peggy) Keevil of the Grims who sparked the author's passion over forty years ago; to the late Mrs Audrey Parlby of the Huckworthy whose knowledge of breeding we shall miss; to the late John Miller whose researches inspired the author to undertake the book. The book used material of the Master of Basset Hounds Association (MBHA), *Baily's Hunting Directories*, *Hounds* magazine, the Surrey Records Office, the National Trust (Clandon House), the English Kennel Club (KC) library, Mrs Margaret Rawle, Mr James Williams, Mr Jim Scharnberg and numerous Masters and followers of basset packs in this country and France.

Additional abbreviations have been used. MFHA: Masters of Foxhounds Association. AMHB: Association of Masters of Harriers & Beagles. BHC: Basset Hound Club. SCC: Sociétié de canine Centrale. FCI: Fedération de cynologique internationale.

Some conventions used: the term 'Basset Hound' is used only for hounds of that specific breed. All specific 'pure' breeds of basset are designated by capitalising the breed name, e.g. Basset Artésien-Normand.The words 'basset' and 'basset hound' are used either when more than one type of basset is being referred to or where there is cross breeding or where the actual breed is unknown or when no formal written breed standards exists. Where an individual hound was KC registered prior to 1918, the registration code, if known, appears in brackets after the name.Where an individual hound is registered with the MBHA, the last two digits of the registration year are shown after the name, preceded by an apostrophe.

No doubt there are numerous errors and omissions in the book. The errors are by accident or lack of information. The omissions are probably from ignorance, sometimes personal bias. Corrections should be aimed at the author, not the publisher, Richard Denny. Without Richard's commitment and enthusiasm, the book would never have got outside the computer.

Chapter Two

Bothering with Bassets

THIS is my personal statement on hunting with bassets. There must be nearly as many reasons why people hunt as there are people. I am no exception. I try to be tolerant of other peoples' views on hunting and on bassets, even when I strongly disagree with them. I hope that you, dear reader, will be as tolerant to me, even when you deem some of my statements to be outrageous!

As a professional researcher, I was taught to try to discover the background of an author, to put the writing into context and appreciate from whence the writer was coming. At the expense of boring you, but to save you the trouble of trying to guess my past, let me indulge myself by a bit of personal reminiscing. You are welcome to skip the next few paragraphs!

My early years in the 1930s and 1940s are a blur of constantly moving between town and country. The periods of stability and peace that predominate my memories are all associated with the countryside and with animals. It was my mother who came from a country background who instilled my love of it. I also remain eternally grateful to my parents for sacrificing so much to my education. These schools endowed me with an excitement of discovery and encouraged me to pursue my interest in the Natural Sciences. They also nurtured my interest in rowing and athletics which led me to coaching. After a period of working on farms, I went to Nottingham University and, just, gained a degree in Chemistry and Botany. But after my National Service, I entered industry and pursued a career in operational research and IT.

Soon after we were married in 1960, we acquired our first Basset Hound. Fortunately whilst exercising him, I met Michael Fulford-Dobson who soon got me whipping-in that winter to the BHC Pack, the nucleus of which were Peggy Keevil's Grims. At about the same time, I was invited to start beagling with the West Surrey and Horsell Beagles. In 1965 we moved to Norfolk and I was able to whip in to John Graham's remarkable pack of hare hounds developed from Bloodhound, Kerry beagle and Dumfriesshire foxhound. In 1967 we returned to Surrey and I hunted the bassets during periods in which John Evans was ill. During the Foot and Mouth outbreak, we spent much time at the Grims kennels helping with hounds and exercising them. By then, Miss Keevil had begun to disband the Grims. When she broke with the BHC, I went with some of her drafts to the newly formed Leadon Vale, later becoming Joint Master for three years. Then petrol shortages prevented me travelling from Surrey to Gloucestershire and for three years I was a Joint Master of the Surrey and North Sussex Beagles. But bassets remained our passion and we returned to them.

My experiences with the beagles were invaluable. Perhaps above all, I had the privilege of working in kennels, in the field and in the show ring with a truly professional Kennel Huntsman, the late Gordon Laing. I was also able to absorb much about the running of a large and long established Hunt: the expectations of followers and the concerns of farmers, landowners and shoots. It also made me think about the differences in hunting with beagles and with bassets.

Family holidays included travelling in France where we became hooked on 'vénerie' and French hounds. We were fortunate to meet Hubert Desamy, the third generation of breeders of all sizes of Griffon Vendéen hounds. My abiding memory of this most remarkable man is of him describing how he decided when to hunt. *'I get up, open the window, breathe in the air and say "Hubert, it is a good day to hunt". I get out my hounds, go into the village and blow a few "fanfare". Those that want to come hunting, come hunting. Those that don't, stay at home!'* Through the late Donald Forbes, we also started to go on hunting trips in France and have continued to do so ever since. This led us to going to Hunt Festivals and then Brevet (hunting trials), as well as making many hunting friends with a variety of hounds, often accompanying the huntsman into the forests. These experiences have led us to appreciate aspects of hunting which are very different to those in the UK.

By keeping in touch with Peggy Keevil when she retired to Exmoor, we were introduced to the Devon and Somerset Staghounds. We had the privilege of seeing at close quarters the professional huntsman and his 'tufters'. From these experiences, we learnt much more about drawing and casting with hounds. Retirement and the children having left home allowed us to go out with more and more packs of beagles, harriers, stag hounds and bassets.

Our continuing love affair with bassets is not just through loyalty. Having seen most types of hound and hunting, the hare still fascinates and surprises us. Maybe it is because so much of a hunt can be seen, the hare tending to run in circles and experience guiding us as to where to go next, or to stay put. Much is because the hare is intelligent and constantly working out new ruses to throw off hounds. Maybe it is the lovely and varied country hares inhabit, from high mountain, through woods and forests, to pasture, to marshland and even the vineyards of Cognac. Why, then, ask our beagling friends in particular, bother with bassets?

David Mann of the Leadon Vale once replied: *'Some people like a good bitter, others a Beaujolais. Whilst I appreciate their tastes, I prefer Champagne.'* To me it is their style. It is their nose, persistence and preciseness. It is their individuality. It is their cry. It is their love of people and life. It is their gentleness. All these allow the basset to be closest to what I consider to be the essence of 'vénerie' in foot hunting.

Note that I say 'allow'. Too often bassets, and beagles, are not encouraged to hunt in their own style. If the objective of the exercise is to race across the country, why use bassets when a pack of beagles give you much greater speed? If the objective of the exercise is measured by the number of hares accounted for, then a gun pack or harriers will produce a much larger tally! Ortho Paget, one of the greatest authorities there has ever been on hunting, said: *'If hounds, be they Beagle or Basset, killed oftener than once in three hunting days they were too big for the country and that one to three ratio was ideal.'* Today, our prime concern in hunting should be how to conserve hares and the environment, not how to destroy them.

The basset's greatest asset lies in its close integration of intelligence and highly sensitive nose. I stress this integration. It is an essential feature. To use it to the full, the basset must be allowed to hunt in a fashion which maximises the outcome of this integration. By its anatomical nature, the basset can only work, relative to other hounds, slowly with its head down for sufficiently long periods for it to detect and analyse complex and sometimes tenuous scent. The basset tends to be an individual worker and self reliant. This results in a pack working over a greater area than expected of most beagle packs. In a draw, the larger coverage of this compensates for the slower speed of progress.

Only too often, the field will press too hard on bassets. This pressure can also be caused by unnecessary movement or impatience from the huntsman or, even worse, by whips. Indeed, there is a growing tendency towards this in the beagle field. Hounds have keen hearing and a wider visual area than Man and one which is geared to detect movement. They are also trained to respond to the commands, often by movements, of the huntsman and whips. As a consequence, anybody moving near them will take some of their attention. This can easily cause them to look up and lose concentration. If bassets realise that the distraction is not helping them and that it has happened several times, they may then 'sulk', virtually saying 'if you know better than me, then get on with it yourself!' Getting bassets' heads down again can be a difficult task and one which only the huntsman can do. He will have difficulty in doing this if he is in the habit of either pressing them too much or not being up with them.

The other reason why I get so annoyed with the field pressing hounds is that hares frequently let hounds go right over them or can sit so tight in a form that hounds do not notice them on the first sweep over a field. Spoiling ground not fully drawn is, in my book, a hanging offence as it probably has spoilt more hunts than anything else I know. Incidentally, it is also much more helpful to the hard-pressed farmer of today to walk the headlands than to trample across a field. It also means that the cover of the hedge makes your movements less obvious to hounds and to hidden hares and is less likely to disturb cattle in adjoining fields.

I have stressed the integration of intelligence and nose. The basset is a very individualistic hound and prefers to work away from others. Contrast this with the beagle who, if not sure, will 'consult' his neighbour. The basset will not do this so readily. At best he will 'feather', but this is more from excitement than a sign to others. What he should do is to give tongue when he is sure. Because of their method of hunting, it is vital that a basset giving tongue can be believed by both his fellow hounds and the hunt staff. They both must be sure that it has a line and that it is a hare, not rabbit, fox or deer. Once again, this surety can be destroyed, usually permanently, by hounds being pressed or unduly hurried or urged on. Once a hound feels that there is urgency to move on, it may resort to giving tongue incorrectly as it wants to please the huntsman. This will lead to further disaster as the other hounds begin to take no notice of it as they realise that it is not reliable. One result is frequent splitting of the pack, some distrusting the offender, others thinking it is the right thing to do. Hence the reason why it is essential to give bassets space, quiet and time to use their intelligence to fully analyse the scent before deciding to give tongue.

Which leads me to another aspect, the number of hounds taken out. The more hounds that are taken out, the greater area they will cover and the greater the risk that one or more will go to fault. There is also a growing likelihood that there will be a few hounds ahead and some trailing behind. This greater spread will mean that the huntsman has greater difficulty in assessing what all the hounds are doing and how much reliance to put on the movements of any individual. It will also mean that each hound has a greater visual and auditory difficulty in keeping in touch with the pack. Possibly more seriously, a large number of hounds inevitably means a few fast hounds. These will quickly alter the nature of the hunting. As they forge ahead from the others, more and more of the other hounds will have to bring their heads up to see where to go and will lose their concentration as they strive to catch up. If this keeps on happening, they will learn to keep looking up so as to anticipate a change in pace and to keep up more easily. Soon many will spend more and more of their time looking rather than scenting. In turn, this may encourage the faster hounds to take the easy option in the field and hunt more by sight than by scent or, worse still, run in the hope of getting a view. It is relevant to this aspect that foot hunting in France rarely exceeds six to eight couple and is often confined to four or five, especially with bassets. It would seem to me that, given the greater prevalence of deer, the spread of rabbit and the increases in hares, there is a yet another reason for taking out fewer hounds. The argument that leaving hounds in kennels without exercise seems to me to say more about kennel management and hound relations than it does about the skills of hunting.

This gives a nice lead in to the vexed subject of rioting and steadiness. Bassets and beagles can be trained to be true and steady. But it takes a lot of consistent time and effort from the huntsman and the hunt staff. Without the continuous influence of a full-time kennel huntsman, this is very difficult to achieve. Without a closely knit, dedicated, fit and knowledgeable team of hunt staff willing to give time at kennels out of season to exercise and to learning hound handling techniques, it is almost impossible to achieve. On top of all this, hound breeding has to be undertaken with great care and research and culling or drafting must be ruthless. Young hounds can only learn from older hounds. Like children, rioting is exciting, especially if led by the adults! It is also mentally easier. You don't have to work on your own and interpret difficult scent. You just have to watch the leader and respond. In watching, you might spot yourself something worth starting a riot for and earn yourself some brownie points from your kennel mates. With a bit of luck, you may have an inexperienced field that will cheer you on. Choose a rabbit for best effect. The field may not spot the difference and you will be declared a 'good' hound! It's good to be popular!

There is no substitute for exercising hounds with plenty of whips in areas known to have hazards. Take out a few hounds at a time. Let the whips surround them as they exercise, but not press them. As soon as a hound looks up at a hazard, a whip should get at the offender. Now here is another difference to beagles. The whip should not rate the hound. Get him to isolate or even hold the hound. The huntsman should then come over as the whips hold up the other hounds. The huntsman should then deal with the hound. One effective way is to lift the hound off, or nearly off, the ground at its shoulders and speak in an angry tone, looking the hound in the eyes, perhaps with some shaking. Let the other hounds see this punishment and shaming taking place. In contrast, when exercising, the huntsman should talk quietly to individual hounds, addressing them by name. The whips should control quietly, again using hound names and directing by movement of the whip and hands, without shouting or cracking the whip. These are the inducements to behave and the punishment for not behaving. Bassets have a loathing of noise and want to be friends with everyone. They will go away from noise if they can and will avoid people they do not trust or like. They have the intelligence to work out what pleases a huntsman and will go out of their way to satisfy as they deem best.

Having said all that, rioting and changing will take place, especially if the country hunted has a surfeit of hares, rabbits, foxes or deer. Minimising the number of hounds taken out and keeping them a level pace will help. Having adequate whips who have been briefed by the huntsman and who have been round the country beforehand will help. But, if rioting keeps occurring, the only answer is to stop hunting for the day or to move to another area, walking the hounds over to settle them down in the manner of exercising suggested in the last paragraph. Allowing rioting to continue will only ensure that it will happen more frequently in the future and be learnt by the new entry. Better to take hounds home, explaining carefully to the field and the land owner, than to perpetuate it. A pack can be ruined in one season. It will take many seasons to re-build.

And this leads me to consider the number of hounds in kennels. The economics of present day hunting, especially where hounds are kept at livery with another Hunt, together with shortages of puppy walkers, mitigate against having large numbers of hounds in kennels and several litters. This is more of a problem for bassets than for beagles. The reason lies in the fact that the basset is a much more unstable breed having originated from more than one type of rough and smooth haired French hound and various outcrosses within the last fifty years. It is also the result of one or more genetical mutations. It is highly likely that some or all of a litter will be too tall or too long or too small or with a weak front, feet or back. It is also likely that a significant number will not have deep noses or good voices or intelligence or even the instinct to hunt. This means that the percentage that should be culled is much greater than with beagles or foxhounds. In turn, this means more litters to give choice. The ideal numbers can be judged by the Grims where Peggy Keevil had over fifty couple or the Walhampton/Westerby who had as many or the late Audrey Parlby who had over twenty couple for a relatively small pack of the Huckworthy hunting only once a week.

What this does mean is that breeding must be carefully worked out to minimise the risks. Also it is essential that a Hunt maintains a consistent breeding policy, not introducing new strains, especially outcrossed stock, more than necessary. Fortunately, bassets are relatively easy to draft or retire as pets, even if they have defects for hunting. But that does mean that followers, supporters and friends should be encouraged to get to know hounds so that there is a constant pool of goodwill that can be used to dispose of hounds. Getting them to help with exercise out of season is one good way of getting this involvement, as well as talking about an individual hound before moving off at each meet. Nobody will then want to have a hound which they know put down because it can not or will not hunt or has got too old.

In France, the problems of keeping sufficient numbers in kennels have arisen through their very stringent rules on kennels and the costs of permits, on top of the laws, restrictions, licences and charges for hunting. Over recent years, the costs associated with kennels have caused many packs to cease to breed most of their litters and to rely on professional breeders. This is made much easier outside the UK because most hounds, and probably all bassets, are bred to written Standards and registered as pure bred with the national Kennel Club. This is possible because there is no separation of showing from working. Consequently, a breeder has a wide market from pet owners, through show and trial enthusiasts to hunts or shoots. The down side is the risk that the breed club becomes dominated by the show enthusiasts, especially those in it for money. This can lead to the dominance of stock which is deemed good for showing, but which is unsuited for working. At the worst, this dominance can, and has, resulted in changes of the written Standard to the detriment of the hunting needs. In France, the SCC work very hard to protect the hunting characteristics within the Standards of breeds internationally recognised as being of French origin. This applies to most basset breeds. The exception is the Basset Hound. This is recognised by the FCI as being English.

Lifting bassets is a very special art which should be used as infrequently as possible with bassets and only in extreme necessity. It requires the concentration of each hound to be broken and their heads to be raised. If it is done too quickly, hounds still puzzling out the line will resent the interference and may not work again that day. 'If you know better, why employ me?' If lifting takes place, it must be done quietly. Once there is the attention of every hound, the huntsman should move off with assurance and purpose, but without undue excitement. Rushing and shouting will increase the time needed to get hounds to concentrate again, rather than watching the huntsman. The time gained in moving them at speed will soon be lost in getting their heads down again.

Allied to lifting is the other art of drawing. An art which seems to be dying out under the pressure of fields demanding constant action and wanting to press on. An art which requires great patience and a very special understanding between huntsman and hounds. It is quite possible to train a pack to draw a complete field backwards and forwards whilst the huntsman remains standing in one spot watching his hounds and directing them by hand movements and a gentle voice. So often this is thwarted by followers walking over the field or distracting hounds by talking. Without careful drawing, hares will be left in the hedgerows or tight in their forms. If fields are not thoroughly drawn and the huntsman gets into the habit of taking hounds through fields until he accidentally hits a line, hounds are more likely to start hunting by sight. Furthermore, if hares are scarce, they will not be found and hounds will be become bored. Bassets seem to get bored much more readily than beagles. That is when rioting is most likely to start.

Dear Reader, you have been so patient. Could you pass me another brick or two? I still have a need to throw some more!

I regret to say the field these days present me with ever more targets. Why is it that gossip is best swapped in gateways and gaps in hedges? Hasn't anybody told them that a hare finds it easier to go through a gateway or gap than squeezing out, in a hurry, elsewhere on to a route it doesn't know so well? Imagine the panic she feels when she approaches a well tried line only to see or hear it occupied by humans! No wonder she stops giving off scent. Imagine too, the frustration that a huntsman feels when hounds check on a line which suddenly changes direction and even has no scent, simply because his hare was headed. All the time and ground gained by the hounds and his skill is lost for want of gossip in the wrong place. A hanging offence, I think.

Pass the next brick, please. I have another member or two of the field in view, or rather hearing. These are those who will talk when hounds or hares are near them, together with those that will holloa at the top of their voices. Up come the hounds' heads and the basset ceases to do what we have bred them for. How a huntsman can tell anything useful from an instant noise, often from an invisible point, I do not know. Raise your hat or your stick and wave it about. But do this after the hare has gone by, so as not to distract her. Try to get over to tell a whip or the huntsman, if he is not in with hounds. If not, when you have his attention, signal the direction in which 'puss' has gone. You may then have the satisfaction of seeing hounds working towards you. Get out of the way of the hounds and let them get on with the job. There is something to be said for the old habit of always turning your back on hounds as they pass by. Don't feel annoyed if the huntsman appears to ignore you. He is in charge and may have other ideas or may not want to go on the country you are indicating. Imagine how annoying and worrying it is if your hounds are holloa'd on to another hare or, worse still, into uncleared country or with cattle in calf or sheep in lamb. Incidentally, I will need two bricks if the offender is blowing a whistle. These have no place in the tranquillity of the countryside! They strictly belong to the football field, along with the rattles.

A few observations on whipping-in. In general, the less I see of them, the better I believe they are playing their part as team member under the captaincy of the huntsman. That implies that there should be a team plan for the day, tactics and constant review through dialogue between huntsman and whips. It also implies that each whip keeps fit enough to be able to keep up with, control and protect the hounds from the first draw to vanning up at the end. Although bassets are relatively slow, they can move faster than most people can run, especially up hill. So the old beagling rule of getting to the top and not coming down too soon is just as essential with bassets as with beagles. Trying to be the extra eyes of the huntsman is a good principle, covering the areas which he, or the field, can not see. To do this, you must anticipate the hounds and think like a hare. How would you set about escaping? One bit of advice I was given which is always helpful is to know or immediately find out where you can get out of a field once you have entered it. This can save invaluable time in a hurry or emergency. The field can also help by not engaging whips in conversation during the hunt.

Relations with hounds is a difficult one. Whips are there to assist the huntsman, not to act as temporary or secondary huntsmen. Apart from being the additional eyes, you are there to turn hounds either to the huntsman or away from hazards. This you can only do by being or by getting in front of hounds, remembering that they can move faster than you can. That means anticipation. Turning does not usually mean cracking your whip and shouting. Either of these will further excite hounds and bring heads up allowing the basset to move even faster. In woods, shouting, as opposed to calling, is most likely to let them know where you are so that they can escape you more easily. If your hound exercise in the summer is well planned and executed, hounds will know that directing with your whip in front of them means 'go back' or 'this way'. Quietly talking to them by name will build a bond with you, leading them to want to please you. That can be a lovely relationship. Being afraid of you simply encourages them to avoid and escape you.

When I started hunting, it was common to have a Field Master, whose word was law and the penalty for disobeying was to be asked to go home. Given the right person, a Field Master would not only make sure that the field gave the best support to the huntsman and cause least damage to the hosts crops, hedges and gates, he imparted knowledge that enhanced one's hunting experience that day and thereafter. Sadly, such posts are now resented by many people who dislike being told what to do. Furthermore, Hunt Committees, worried about maintaining income, are fearful of upsetting or offending followers. The result, in my opinion, is poorer hunting and much greater strains on the huntsman. The Masters of old would simply order people home if they interfered with hunting. But these Masters paid for the hunt and could call the tune. Now we must rely on 'educating' the field. And this means spending time and money on communication, an ability sadly lacking in many Hunts.

Cry is, possibly, the greatest asset of the basset, a legacy from their French origins and hunting in woodland. Sadly, it has been diminished in other types of hounds in England. Not so in Europe, largely because so much hunting is still in deep forest where cry is absolutely essential to stay in contact with hounds. There is the lovely story of a Master several centuries ago who sent, as a present, a couple to another Master some two days journey away. They were returned some days later with a courteous note thanking him for the present but regretting that he had no vacancies at present in his pack for any more tenors!

It is worth just considering why the basset can produce such a lovely, bell-like, voice. It requires depth in the chest, throat and head to produce the necessary power and resonance. Unlike when a hound sings, the head tends to be down when it starts. Here is yet another reason why it is so important for bassets to be hunted with their heads down. The greatest danger is the alteration of body and head structure through outcrossing with other breeds. In my opinion, no advantage gained in other particulars from outcrossing is worth diminution in voice, especially if it is likely to be accompanied by a smaller skull and a smaller area for the mucous membranes and, hence, scenting capabilities.

Fronts and feet are, or should be, a constant concern with bassets. There is a dilemma. The weight, length and size of the hound requires a large chest to adequately house a heart and lungs of sufficient power. This has to be carried between front legs that are shortened by being a basset. If the legs, in relation to the length, are not short, then the hound should not be classified as basset and probably will not have a basset genetical profile. As a consequence, the foreleg may be crooked to a greater or lesser extent (to virtually straight) to clear the chest side and the forefeet will have a tendency to turn out for balance. All is made more hazardous because the bone development process in a basset creates a much thicker and spongier formation of the leg joints. This increases the risk of 'knuckling over' and 'cow hocking', both of which will impede movement at speed and over rough ground. The long back of the basset creates additional strains, especially on the last few vertebra, and can lead to arthritic problems in the leg joints. These strains are made worse if the top line dips in the middle or at the rear, including having a stern put on too low, causing the back to drop away.

These areas are genetically controlled and should play a large part in the selection for breeding as defects can be genetically dominant. Diet and exercise in early months can be important, remembering that bones do not fully calcify for many weeks after whelping. Calcium intake, in an absorbable form, is vital. Care should be taken to avoid puppies jumping off heights or taking too much exercise at any one time. As basset bitches tend to have large litters, the health of the bitch must be closely monitored, especially her intake of adequate protein and minerals. Puppy walkers have an especially vital task with bassets in getting the balance right between too much and too little exercise and providing the right diet.

If this chapter provokes some thought and disagreement, then it will have achieved its objective. The day that there is nothing more to learn or dispute about hunting is the day the final 'Gone Away' and 'Home' should be blown!

Why 'bothering' with bassets? Trying keeping or walking some!

Chapter Three

Types of Basset

It is not the intention of this chapter to detail the history of bassets. Nor is the intention to repeat the International Breed Standards as these are published by the Kennel Club and on the Internet. The aims are to look at historical references to bassets, to introduce the basic hunting and show breeds which exist today in England; to show how these have been developed; and to mention some allied breeds. Detail on developments for hunting will be covered in subsequent chapters devoted to individual hunts and people.

Historical References

Many cave drawings and paintings from the Middle East, especially from Egypt, Greece and the Roman Empire, are said to represent bassets. Similarly, there are many medieval paintings, tapestries and carvings in stone and wood which can be interpreted as featuring bassets. One example is in Cotehele House in Cornwall where there is a fourteenth century Welsh wooden carving of hounds and a hare. The evidence put forward is largely based upon the carvings showing long-bodied and, sometimes, short-legged, hounds with pendulous ears. This evidence is not very convincing. Drawings and paintings were more symbolic and stylised than accurate until well into the Renaissance. Lengthening of the body of an animal and giving it short legs was common in art up until the nineteenth century. One only has to look at eighteenth century paintings of racehorses and cattle to see this.

Some historic texts are also quoted as early evidence of bassets. One favourite is from William Shakespeare's *A Midsummer Night's Dream*, written about 1598. A speech describes a hound with long ears, having dew laps, slow, with a bell-like voice and crooked legs. It may also elude to the method of hunting by ending in the phrase '*each on each*'. Once again, there is no objective evidence that these refer to bassets. Representations and texts, even if of long-backed hounds, could equally as well have been based upon the St Hubert hound or its derivatives, the Talbot and the Bloodhound. They could also be based upon ancestors of the Dachshund as upon a basset. Modern research indicates that Dachshunds and Bloodhounds are genetically different to bassets.

However, as will be seen in a later chapter, the genetic causes of 'bassetism' are genetic mutations with a relatively high incidence rate. Furthermore, it is known that this group of mutations occur in many species, including Man. They must have occurred frequently throughout the evolutionary history of the dog. Indeed, the indications are that almost all of the regional hound types in Europe, at some time or another, had basset varieties. The important question is not whether they occurred. The questions are when were these mutants first deliberately kept by Man; when did Man first encourage this 'basset' trait in the breeding of hounds; and what caused Man to make these decisions?

The first use of the word 'basset' with a detailed description is contained in Jacques du Fouilloux's book of about 1573. Almost at the beginning of Chapter LX on 'The Hunting of Foxes and Tessons', he uses the word 'Basset' and goes on to describe two types. He suggests that one type came from the region of Flandre and the other the region of Artois. He specifically says that the Flandre type had crooked legs and a short coat whilst the Artois had straight legs and a rough coat, like the 'barbets', a griffon-like hound. He says that the Flandre type was used underground for badgers (one of the Tesson group of quarry) as well as for foxes because they were always wanting to fight. He contrasts this with the Artois type which he says were used above ground and possessed very great passion and audacity. He then goes on to give very detailed instructions as to how to bring up and train bassets.

In Chapter LXII, he includes a section entitled 'How to deploy the Bassets according to the earths which are found'. From all this we gather that bassets were used on fox, wolf, boar and badger. He also describes how a noble should accompany his hounds.

> A Noble should have a little cart, where inside this there should be a young girl, ideally sixteen to seventeen years old, who can massage your head on the way. You should have a half dozen monks, to counter earthly thoughts, at the end to take the Bassets to the abbey: or just wanting to take some good plain air, as one can in this way. Have made in it a fur suit, of a simple type, and grand sized mattress, and that sewn up so it can also subtly be a bale: for then when it is folded up from side to side, it will make a seating place for a little snack, like a bale or a bagpipe, which is made up in the same way when the wind is in it, then fill it up with a syringe or have a good pair of bellows, made like the one used by a goldsmith. All the inside and the coverings of the cart should be stocked with flagons and bottles, and have at the end of the cart a wooden trunk, plenty of cold Indian chicken, hams, beef tongues, and other good edibles. And if it is winter weather, you must take your little pavilion, and make a fire in this , or dress well in a robe like the Nymphe.

Along with evidence from the wood cuts in this sixteenth century book, Fouilloux gives us the first firm evidence of the uses of bassets in hunting. The two types described were almost certainly the ancestors of our present day smooth and rough haired bassets, the former often with crooked legs and the latter usually straight legged. He indicates that bassets were kept because of their scenting abilities, tenacity and aggression. The book also suggests that the smooth haired were primarily for working underground and the rough haired for working above ground. However, this is only the statement of one man from the northern regions of France. We have no firm evidence that his accounts of use were true throughout France.

The First French Revolution in 1789 led to the demise of hunting in France. It was revived under the new Constitution of 1794 which gave every citizen the right to hunt on their own land. But it was not until after the Second Revolution of 1815 that the French felt able to hunt again. By then, most of the French breeds of hound had been lost. It was not until the mid 1800s that serious attempts were made to revive some of the breeds.

The basis of modern bassets was due to the work of one man, the Comte le Couteulx de Canteleu. His work is described in more detail in a later chapter. His publication in 1858 marks the point from which we have detailed factual information about the creation, breeding and uses of bassets. In 1852, he set about re-creating the traditional French hounds. It was at this time that the ideas of pure bred dogs was arising in the growing hobby of 'dog fancying'. He later wrote that he found that many breeds,

Earliest drawing of a hound referred to as a basset and illustrating the recommended mode of transport. Jacques du Fouilloux, 1573.

including the bassets, had almost entirely disappeared. He managed to find a Griffon Vendéen dog and used a wolf bitch. From this and other experiments, he managed to breed a pack. He may have been helped by the creation of the rough haired Fauve de Bretagne by Baron Joseph de Carayon la Tour in about 1840.

In his book, Couteulx described two types of basset. One was with short legs, long back, long ears, a lovely head and voice and used for rabbit and hare. The other type was rough haired and used for roe deer, wolf and boar. Both were straight legged. The rough haired appear to have been rare. He found bassets easy to breed. He also says that there were other crooked legged varieties. One of these may have been the Basset Allemande, which are now thought to have been the ancestors of the modern Dachshund.

In the early 1860s, the Comte turned his attentions away from rough haired hounds to smooth haired. He bred substantial numbers of these as bassets, with both straight and crooked legs. It was the latter that were imported into England in 1866. Over the next thirty-five years many more bassets were imported into England from France, including rough coated in 1870.

Basic Breeds of Bassets

Most literature refers to five basic breeds of present day bassets, one in two sizes. These are:

- The smooth haired Basset Artésien-Normand
- The smooth haired Basset Bleu de Gascogne
- The rough haired Basset Griffon Vendéen, Grand and Petit
- The rough haired Basset Fauve de Bretagne
- The smooth haired Basset Hound

There are, or have been, a number of other breeds that some authorities classify as bassets. They include:

Alpine Basset
(Alpine Dachsbracke, Alpenländische Dachsbracke, Mantano-Alpine Dachsbracke)
Baden Basset
Basset Ardennais
Basset d'Artois
(Basset Française d'Artois, Basset St Hubert au Ardenais)
Basset de Flandre
Basset de Saintonge
Basset Griffon Nivernais
Bernese Basset
(Berner Niederflaufhund)
Burgos Basset
Danish Basset
(Danish Dachsbracke)
Hungarian Basset
Ilyrian Basset
Jura Basset
Lucerne Basset
(Schwyz Basset, Schwyzer Niederlaufhund, Swiss Niederlaufhunde)
Massicks
Normand Basset
(Basset de Normandie)
St. Domingos Basset
Swedish Drever
(Swedish Beagle, Swedish Dachsbracke)
Westphalian Basset
(Sauerland Basset Hound, Sauerlander Dachsbracke, Westphalian Dachsbracke)

The five basic breeds, together with the three listed above and shown in *italics*, are breeds recognised internationally. All of them are used for hunting in Europe, predominantly to the gun.

In England, most Hunts have found it necessary to outcross these pure breeds in order to have a hound that will hunt for several hours a day for up to three days every week in the hunting season. Hunts in more difficult countries (fen, moor, mountain) have also found it necessary to outcross to produce a hound able to cope with these harsh terrains. A few Hunts have tried to maintain a pack of pure bred hounds, notably the Grims, Rallye Beauvautrait, Albany and Black Mountain. The latter two are still active but both have recently found it necessary to outcross.

The main outcrosses for hunting can be divided into three types, the word 'basset' being used with a small 'b' to denote a non pure-bred type:

- The smooth haired English basset
- The smooth haired Anglo-Artésien-Normand basset
- The rough haired Anglo-Vendéen basset

The five 'pure bred' and the three cross bred hunting types are now briefly described. More detailed descriptions and histories of the five pure-breeds can be found in Booth's book of 2002 (USA), Leblanc's and Miller's book of 1987 (France) and Johnston's book of 1968 (England). Details of the cross-breeding for hunting can be found in subsequent chapters.

Basset Artésien-Normande

A smooth coated, semi-crooked basset with a dark tricolour coat and of slim build, with features and characteristics of the ancient Normand and Artois hounds of France, 30 to 36 cm high.

In 1858 the Comte le Couteulx de Canteleu described two types of basset, rough and smooth. He concentrated his attention on the smooth haired type. The evidence is that the Comte produced two types of smooth basset. One was straight or semi-crook legged and the other fully crooked leg and much heavier and lower. These may have represented his attempts to revive the old Artois and Normand hounds. Whilst the Comte seems to have concentrated upon the straight or semi-crooked legged variety, another breeder, Louis Lane, further developed the heavier, crooked leg type, probably from Couteulx stock. These two varieties appear in the literature under a variety of names. The lighter type, favoured for hunting, were referred to as Couteulx, Artois or Model type. The heavier variety, favoured in France for showing, were referred to as Lane, Normand or Termino type (although the latter may have been a third variety). The better qualities from the two types were brought together by Leon Verrier in the 1870s. This breed became the modern Basset Artésien-Normand.

The Basset Artésien-Normand still has a strong following in France, both for showing and for hunting mainly rabbit, hare and roe deer. The original Couteulx and Lane types were imported into England and were shown during the second half of the nineteenth century. The development of the hound followed radically different paths

Basset Artésien-Normand, Ulema de Barly, inported by Miss Keevil to the Grims in 1946.

in England, compared to France. In France, it has always been regarded primarily as a hound to hunt in small packs, not usually exceeding six couple, and to the gun. The majority of this hunting is in forests and other cover. In England it was imported for use in packs of ten or more couple, solely on hare and without guns and in open country. As a consequence, the Basset Hound was developed in England from the original Basset Artésien-Normand and replaced it as a show breed. Basset Artésien-Normand hounds have been imported into England on a number of occasions throughout the twentieth century, but in small numbers. They have always been used as outcrosses, primarily for hunting, and never bred or shown as a breed since the nineteenth century.

A closely related breed exists, the Chien d'Artois (53 to 58 cm), but is not a basset.

Basset Bleu de Gascogne

A smooth coated, straight legged basset coloured white and black with 'bleu' ticking. Bred to have many of the points and characteristics of the ancient Gascogne and Saintongeois hounds of France, 34 to 38 cm high.

These first appeared in a litter of a cross in 1886 between a Gascogne and a Saintongeois in the Plaisance-Dordogne kennels of Monsieur J.G. Giet. Whether this was by accident or design is still debated. Monsieur Giet was trying to breed a new type of gun dog from the best characteristics of these two traditional French breeds. To this end, he took his stallion Saintongeois, Moniteur, and mated him to pure bred Gascogne bitches from the long established Fourmis-Dordogne of Monsieur Piston. In one litter, probably from Misere, there were '*a couple very low to the ground, true bassets.*' He then bred from these 'bassets' and sold them all to a Monsieur d'Heudieres of the Chateau de Bois-David in Normandy. The sale was to enable Monsieur Giet to take on a pack of beagles. He later expressed regret in making this sale.

The words used by Monsieur Giet could indicate that he was not seeking to breed a basset strain. The two original puppies seem to have been unexpected and to have arisen spontaneously. But, in 1893, Monsieur Paul Gerusez, a respected Cynegeticist (study of hunting with dogs) and a connoisseur of bassets, wrote about Monsieur Giet:

Basset Bleu de Gascogne.

'*. . . I think that very probably he knew what the result would be*'. He suggested that Monsieur Giet knew that such crosses sometimes threw bassets, although these were usually put down at birth.

They were not a great success until Monsieur Alain Bourbon in the Mayenne took them up in about 1904. The revival was short lived and the breed almost disappeared until the late 1960s when Monsieur Jean Abadie of Ger began to breed them again, the result being the modern Basset Bleu de Gascogne. Apart from showing, the hound is used mainly for hunting hare and roe deer, usually to the gun or sometimes in small packs.

Until 1996 the Basset Bleu de Gascogne was hardly known in England. Mr Andrew Spillane imported some, primarily for hunting hare with a pack in East Anglia, the Rallye Beauvautrait. They were exhibited at a number of shows. In 2004 the pack was merged with the Black Mountain Hare Hounds in Wales. The numbers of pure Basset Bleu de Gascogne bred in England are limited.

Three other breeds of Bleu de Gascogne exist today: Grand Bleu de Gascogne (65 to 75 cm male), Petit Bleu de Gascogne (52 to 58 cm male), and Griffon Bleu de Gascogne (50 to 57 cm male). The latter is rough coated.

Basset Griffon Vendéen

A rough coated, straight legged basset of pale grey, fawn or tricolour colour and with a griffon head, this is the largest of the bassets. Bred for the characteristics of the ancient Vendéen hounds. Now exists in two sizes.

It is possible that these bassets survived the French Revolution as the Vendée was an isolated and very independent Region that fought for its independence. Certainly, in 1858, the Comte le Couteulx found a single Griffon Vendéen dog. He described rough haired, straight legged bassets which he had and used for roe deer, wolf and boar. He said that they were rare. By the end of the century the Basset Griffon Vendéen was

Basset Griffon Vendéen.

well established for hunting and showing, thanks to the efforts of the Comte d'Elva and the Vicomte de Villebois-Mareuil. One family, the Desamy (or Dézamy) were greatly responsible for the development of this breed, even to the beginning of the 21st century. Initially, Paul Desamy created a 42 cm basset which became the Breed Standard. He was succeeded by his son, Paul Desamy, who unfortunately died in 1933, but was replaced by his son, Abel Desamy. Abel rescued and built up the breed after the War from the few surviving examples. Hubert, his son, carried on the work.

During the 1940s, growing interest was shown in smaller specimens of the Basset Griffon Vendéen, not only for hunting rabbit, as opposed to hare or deer, but also for showing. In 1951 two standards were agreed. The Petit Basset Griffon Vendéen should be between 34 and 38 cm for males. The larger variety are the Grand Basset Griffon Vendéen.

The Basset Griffon Vendéen was an early import into England and became popular following the Royal Family introducing them into the Sandringham in 1890. Experiments were made with outcrossing them to smooth haired bassets for hunting. But the results were not satisfactory, the rough haired hounds having a tendency to work like terriers, rather than hounds.

In 1938 Rupert Buchanan-Jardine of Lockerbie imported some and, together with some Westerby blood, formed the Castle Milk pack. Some of these survived the War. After the War, Lionel Woolner imported some and used the Castle Milk stock to form the West Lodge Harehounds in Hertfordshire. Some Petit Basset Griffon Vendéen were imported in the late 1960s by a well known breeder of Basset Hounds, Mrs Mildred Sieffert. They have now become popular for showing. Some descendents of these were acquired by Nick Valentine in 1974, together with some Westerby hounds with Castle Milk bloodlines. From these, he formed a pack in Herefordshire, the Bradley Vale, now the Ryeford Chase. Some of these were acquired by John Williams in 1998 and formed the basis of the Black Mountain.

Two other Vendéen breeds exist today, the Grand Griffon Vendéen (62–68 cm, male) and the Briquet Griffon Vendéen (50–55 cm, male).

Basset Fauve de Bretagne

The smallest and most compact of the bassets (32 to 38 cm) with a hard, rough coat coloured from wheaten to a deep fawnish red, with straight or slightly crooked legs, giving them a characteristically swaggering gait.

Thought to be a very old breed from Brittany but which probably became extinct in the early nineteenth century. Appears to have been re-bred at the end of the century from the very ancient Fauve de Bretagne (48 to 56 cm) and the Basset Griffon Vendéen. Whilst they were bred in the 1890s by Monsieur Monti de Rézé and by Monsieur Alain Bourbon just before the First World War, they never became popular in France, being overshadowed as a rough coated basset by the Basset Griffon Vendéen. It was not until 1921 that a Breed Standard was established in France. Now they are very popular in France, both for showing and hunting with a gun and as a pack.

From time to time a few have been introduced into England. But it was only towards the end of the twentieth century that they began to appear at shows. Nick Valentine introduced some to his Ryeford Chase pack in 1980. No other pack of hunting hounds in England is known to have used them. This may be because they are excitable and have, compared to other bassets, a poor voice. Being small, they are more adapted to hunting rabbit than hare.

There are two related breeds: the Fauve de Bretagne (48 to 55 cm, male) and the

Basset Fauve de Bretagne.

Griffon Nivernais (55 to 62 cm, male). The latter has a mainly charcoal coat with the fawn confined to the head.

Basset Hound

A smooth coated, crook legged basset of heavy and low build with many of the features of the Basset Artésien-Normand, 33–38 cm high. They are generally tricolour, sometimes bicolour, although any hound colour is acceptable. The only basset to be developed in England. It was not recognised in France until 1950, but became very popular in the United States from the 1930s.

The breed was created at the end of the nineteenth century by outcrossing the original Basset Artésien-Normand with Bloodhound and with the hunting stock of basset developed by Godfrey Heseltine in his Walhampton pack. The breed was developed for showing and was only favoured occasionally by the Hunts as an outcross. Between the Wars, it almost died out in England as a show dog due to its poor physique. It was due to three breeders, Mrs Elms, Mrs Grew and Miss Keevil, that it survived. In the 1940s Miss Keevil set about reviving and improving the Basset Hound at her kennels near Newbury. This she achieved by judicious outcrossing with Westerby and Wick hunting bassets and Mrs Elms's Reynalton Bloodhounds. She also imported and used two Basset Artésien-Normand from France. The resultant Basset Hound proved to be popular in shows, as well as being able to hunt hare in her Grims pack. This led to a Breed Standard being adopted by the Kennel Club of Great Britain. However, the development of the Basset Hound in the United States went in the direction of a more heavy hound. As the American market was so large, this heavier standard became the International Standard and was adopted by the Kennel Club of Great Britain in the 1960s.

The Basset Hound to the International Standard survived as a hunting hound by the

Basset Hound. Grims Warlock'46.

formation of the Albany in 1972 by the BHC. However, towards the end of the last century, it was being found in England and in France that this type of Basset Hound was beginning to lose its instinct for hunting. At the same time the type favoured in the show ring had become heavier and lower, with a consequent loss of agility and pace in the field. As a result, the Albany had to outcross with Fourshires and the Huckworthy. In 2003 the BHC decided to cease its support for the Albany and it became independent. No organised fully working packs of Basset Hounds now exist in the UK or Ireland. Only two hunting packs of Basset Hound are currently active in France.

The English basset

A smooth coated basset usually with straight, or almost straight, legs and usually tricolour with many of the characteristics of the Basset Artésien-Normand, but more substantial and with a shorter back, small head and shorter ears. The emphasis is on a frame which is strong and agile.

This hound only exists in working packs of hounds in the British Isles and in North America. It has no written Breed Standard and is not recognised by the Kennel Club or Internationally. It was originally developed by Godfrey Heseltine with his Walhampton pack in the 1890s to the First World War. He and others, including Sir Everett Millais, took the original smooth coated Basset Artésien-Normand and improved it by introducing various outcrosses, the principal ones being Bloodhound and Harrier. The objective was to produce a hound that could hunt all day with speed, drive and agility, but which retained the basset voice. It was the success of this type of hound that led to the split in 1911 between the BHC which favoured the development

English basset. Westerby Gentle. Champion Bitch, MBHA Annual Show, Peterborough, 2000.

of a heavier basset with pronounced crook and a head resembling a Bloodhound. Following the death of Godfrey Heseltine in 1932, the successor to the Walhampton, the Westerby, under the Mastership of Eric Morrison, carried on and further developed the English basset.

From the 1930s to the 1950s, the English basset was almost the only type of basset in England, the BHC being disbanded in 1921 for lack of numbers. It was primarily the English basset that was used after WWII to re-establish the Basset Hound in England. However, just as Miss Keevil had to use outcrosses to re-establish the Basset Hound, Eric Morrison of the Westerby had to use other outcrosses to re-establish the English basset. Once again Harrier blood was used, together with some Foxhound and Fell Hound. With the exception of the Grims and until the 1960s, all the basset packs in England were of the English basset type. On its revival in 1957, the MBHA coined the name 'English basset'. Over the past thirty years, the distinctions between the basset varieties used for hunting in England have become less as all have used other blood lines from time to time. The Westerby remains the main repository of the English basset.

Anglo-Artésien-Normand basset

A smooth coated basset with slightly crooked legs, generally tricolour, but with any hound colour. Retains many of the characteristics of the Basset Artésien-Normand, but more substantial, with less crook and less exaggerated features. The emphasis is on retaining the deep scenting abilities and melodious voice whilst being able to run for long distances and clear obstacles.

Originally bred after WWII by Miss Keevil for her Grims pack. It was this breeding that became the accepted type of Basset Hound in England until the American Standard was adopted internationally in the 1960s On Miss Keevil's withdrawal from hunting and showing, partially as a result of the adoption of the American Standard, she encouraged the formation of two new packs: Fourshires in Oxfordshire and the Leadon Vale in Gloucestershire and drafted to them most of her hunting stock. It was this type of Basset Hound that the Albany tried to preserve for the BHC and Mrs Parlby held in

Anglo-Artésien-Normand basset. Fourshires Governor. Champion Doghound, MHBA Annual Show Peterborough, 1999.

Anglo-Vendéen basset. West Lodge, 1986.

her Huckworthy pack. Over the last forty years, further improvements have been made by all the UK basset Hunts using outcrosses between themselves and other types of working hound. This has resulted in a much more compact and harder form of the Anglo-Artésien-Normand basset, but has retained much of the striking head, ears and voice. In 2003 Jose Jimenz visited England looking for Basset Hounds to improve his pack, La Ciguela, in Spain. It was the Anglo-Artésien-Normand basset from the Huckworthy which he imported.

Anglo-Vendéen-basset

A rough coated basset usually with straight legs, generally light fawn with or without some white, sometimes dark fawn. Generally with a griffon type head and shortish ears and with many of the characteristics of the Basset Griffon Vendéen, from which most of them are descended. Renowned for their determination and aggression in the hunting field and fearlessness of dense cover and thorns. But also known for their independence and tendency to hunt and give tongue on any game that gets up. Their hunting has been described as more akin to that of a working terrier than a hound. Difficult to work in any numbers as a pack.

Rough coated bassets have been imported into England on a number of occasions from 1870 to the present day, both for hunting and as show hounds. In the hunting packs, they have tended to be outcrossed with the Basset Artésien-Normand, the English basset and the Anglo-Artésien-Normand basset. Over the past few years, the Black Mountain have also outcrossed them with the Basset Bleu de Gascogne.

Packs which have had or still have predominantly Anglo-Vendéen bassets include the Castle Milk, the West Lodge, the Bradley Vale and the Black Mountain. The West Lodge have tended to move away towards the English basset type.

Chapter Four

Hunting Development

Hunting with dogs is thought to date back to the early ages of man when he learnt to harness the abilities of wolves to improve his chances of catching wild animals for food. Gradually, he found how to breed and train animals for specific purposes. This process probably evolved at different times and in different ways in more than one part of the world. As a consequence, dogs with good sight and which ran fast were developed as 'gaze' hounds for open country such as the Middle East, North Africa and Russia. For areas with deep forests and scrublands in such areas as Europe, 'scenting' hounds were developed. A natural development in these areas was to breed hounds for specific purposes and specific game. Hounds with enhanced scenting abilities could locate and flush out quarry. Other hounds were bred for stamina and speed to pursue the quarry. Special hounds may have been bred for their fearlessness to bring quarry to bay and to kill it. There may have been different hounds for small quarry such as rabbit, hare and small deer and others for bigger game, such as stag and boar.

Successful types of hounds were probably greatly prized and secrets of their breeding may have been guarded. This, combined with the physical isolation of various tribes, may well have led to regional types of hounds. Individuals may have become recognised in the tribe as specialist hunters with dogs. Possibly their relations with their hounds may have led them to be endowed with a mysticism by their peers. This may have led to the development of rites and of dress or personal decoration. These hunters may have come to occupy a special place in the social organisation of tribes. Their importance is indicated by the fact that primitive stone and cave drawings depict hunters almost as frequently as warriors. Yet those engaged in other activities figure relatively infrequently.

Historians are more and more inclined to believe that pleasure activities occurred relatively early in the history of Man, albeit that some these activities may have been associated with ritual and mysticism. Hunting may well have developed as one such pleasure activity, at the same time as being a means of filling the larder or deterring predators. The ability to control and ride horses would have introduced added dimensions both to pleasure activities and to hunting for food. The speed and endurance of the horse, which have been enhanced by controlled breeding, must have influenced the development of hounds and the rituals of hunting. But the economic requirements for keeping a horse may well have restricted these developments to wealthy and ruling families. Their positions in society may also have given them greater opportunities to indulge in the recreational rather than the food gathering aspects of hunting.

Equally important, social changes have had major influences on the development of types of hounds and hunting practices. Some are of particular importance to the development of hunting with bassets:

- Laws and the French Constitutions
- The Industrial Revolution

- The French Revolution
- The development of transportation
- Collecting and 'fancying'
- The First and Second World Wars
- Agricultural economics and practices
- Firearm developments
- Theories of evolution and genetics
- Royalty and government
- Dog and hunting associations

Many of these influences have interacted with each other. Rather than trying to outline each influence, this Chapter will look at groups of related influences.

Evolution and Genetical Theories

Charles Darwin was born in 1809 and published *On the Origin of Species by Means of Natural Selection or, the Preservation of Favoured Races in the Struggle for Life* in 1859; *The Variation of Animals and Plants Under Domestication* in 1868 and *The Descent of Man, and Selection in Relation to Sex* in 1871. His ideas of evolution had profound effects on society in general and on livestock breeding. But he also argued that acquired characteristics could be inherited and that males were more evolutionarily advanced than females. His ideas were quickly taken up by hound and dog breeders, especially as many of them were well read and interested in the natural sciences. Darwin's work may well have influenced the French in setting up the Jardin d'Acclimatation in Paris in 1860.

In 1895 Sir Everett Millais delivered a lecture at St Thomas's Hospital in London entitled *Two Problems of Reproduction.* This was published by *Our Dogs* which was widely read by people concerned with breeding dogs, including those in hunting. In this lecture he laid down his thinking behind and the results of his crossing of bassets with bloodhounds. It is very clear that Darwin's ideas had heavily influenced Everett's thinking and breeding experiments.

The two basic Laws of Genetics, covering what we now refer to as genes and chromosomes, were enunciated by an Austrian monk, Gregory Mendel, in 1869 in his *Experiments in Plant Hybrids.* But he was obscure and his work remained largely unknown until the early 1900s. In 1900 Carl Erich Correns in Germany published experiments which confirmed Mendel's work, but it was not until after 1902 that he realised that they had been published by Mendel. Also in 1900, Erich Tschermak von Seysenegg reported his findings on experimental plant breeding and that his literature search had uncovered the work of Mendel. Yet a third person, Hugo de Vries at the University of Amsterdam, formulated Laws of Inheritance and attributed the discovery of these to Mendel. Between 1901 and 1903 de Vries discovered spontaneous alterations of characters and coined the word 'mutation'. This work was published as *The Mutation Theory.* Just before the First World War, August Weisman at the University of Freiburg developed a theoretical idea of 'germ plasma', germ cells independent of other body cells. We would now call them chromosomes, genes and DNA. Whilst Weisman was a supporter of Darwin's idea of evolution, he refuted Darwin's idea that acquired characteristics can be inherited.

The publication of these works was not well known outside academic circles. As the papers were not in English, even less notice was probably taken in the UK. So the concept of mutation did not take a hold in UK hound breeding circles and was probably delayed even longer by the onset of the 1914–18 War. As will be seen in Chapter 5, mutation is at the heart of why a basset is a basset.

The science of genetics had been born and developed with ever increasing speed. In 1915 Hermann Muller published *The Mechanism of Mendelian Heredity*. In 1926 he showed that X-rays could cause genetic mutations and that these were the result of chromosomes being broken and that these changed individual genes. Muller was awarded the Nobel Prize in 1946. His work led to interest in inherited diseases and abnormalities in dogs and the creation of registers in breeds of blood lines free of specific known diseases and abnormalities. The BHC was one of the early pioneers in this in the mid 1960s for hip dysplasia. However, this initiative was not taken up by the MBHA and it is not known how widespread this is in hunting bassets.

James Watson and Francis Crick published two papers in 1953 in *Nature* showing how DNA could duplicate itself and, hence, how genes worked. In 1965 Watson published *Molecular Biology of the Gene.* Crick was largely interested in three dimensional structure of large molecules and in 1966 published *Molecules and Man.* Maurice Wilkins had joined the Biophysics Unit of the Medical Research Council in 1946. Here he developed the X-ray diffraction techniques used to unravel the structure of DNA. In 1962, Watson, Crick and Wilkins were awarded the Nobel Prize for their work on DNA. As a result of this, the Human Genome Project was launched and has recently resulted in the publication of a complete map of the human chromosome structure. More recently, the Dog Genome Project has been launched and the first results are beginning to be published. It remains to be seen how this mapping will be used in the hound world. Some specific aspects of both evolution and genetics are discussed in more detail in a Chapter 5.

Land Ownership, Legislation and the World Wars

Hunting is closely linked to the ownership of land. In turn, individual ownership and control of land has, and still is, heavily influenced by state legislation. In feudal times much of the land was owned by the Monarch or by the Church. But subsequent social developments differed between England and France. The result has been dissimilar patterns of land control. This, in turn, led to differing developments of hunting in the two countries, a situation that is evident to this day.

From feudal times there has been another major difference between England and France, partially due to the land mass and the nature of the land. The power in France directly exercised by the monarch or head of state throughout the Kingdom has always been less in France than in England. The French monarchy reigned over a coalition, sometimes unstable, of almost autonomous regional dukedoms. This led to a French Court predominantly powerful in and around Paris, but often with little interest or knowledge of the rest of the country. Contrast this to England in which the Court did move around and the monarch protected his hunting by declaring vast areas to be Royal Forests and imposing the harsh Forest Laws. As the latter were relaxed, the new landowners emulated the monarch by creating enclosed hunting parks in their lands.

In England, the monarchy and church control radically changed in the sixteenth century under Henry VIII when much of the land which he seized from the Church was distributed by him as favours to his supporters. Following the failure of the Commonwealth and the return and rise of Parliamentary government, a new aristocracy arose from within the parliamentary ranks. Many of these invested heavily in land.

The fortunes made in the Industrial Revolution increased the number of landowners. The attractions of land ownership increased as the food demands of a growing urban population pushed up the prices of agricultural produce giving landowners good financial returns on their land, both from the products and from tenancies. The adoption of new agricultural practices increased the crop yields. In addition, all through this period, more and more land was cleared, including the forests.

The result was that each new landowner wanted to show their importance and wealth. This they did by emulating the style of the Court of the time and this included having their own pack of hounds. Whilst stag hunting remained the premier sport, the lack of forest restricted it. Initially, the harrier and hare hunting were favoured. In the eighteenth century fox hunting took over in the desire for more speed and the excitement of the jump. The availability of large tracts of cultivated land also helped development. In the nineteenth century, increases in landowners, some of them on comparatively small scales, and then the enclosures of fields as a result of the Enclosures Acts, led to a resurgence of hare hunting and the use of beagles, a breed developed in England under Queen Elizabeth I and, later, of bassets when they were imported from France.

Whilst guns were first developed in the fourteenth century, they were largely used by the military. It was not until the incorporation of locks in the sixteenth and seventeenth centuries that they became safe enough to be used for non-military purposes in the country. They were expensive and only available to the aristocracy and wealthy land owners. It was not until the end of the eighteenth century when the percussion lock became available that guns were safe and cheaper enough for more widespread use. In the mid nineteenth century the percussion lock guns were superseded by the breach loaded gun. In France at the beginning of the nineteenth century the gun became the most effective means of controlling the ever increasing numbers of wolves and wild boar. These increases were, in part, due to the banning of hunting following the First Revolution. Some authorities proposed that the basset was developed to drive game to gun, the existing hounds being too fast. They also suggest another reason for needing a slow hound was the long time needed to re-load these barrel loading guns. Hunting with hounds 'à Tir' remains very popular in France to this day, but was never taken up in England. Instead, breeds of gun dogs were developed from non-hunting strains.

Increasingly during the nineteenth and twentieth centuries shooting has played an increasing part in the economy of the countryside in the UK. In the nineteenth century shooting (and hunting) rights were kept by the land owner even when the land was tenanted for farming. These rights became an important source of income for land owners when the agricultural recession of the 1870s struck. The sporting rights became attractive assets in selling land to the new moneyed classes who chose to live in the country and work in the cities as a result of the railway.

During the last few decades, shooting has become a major commercial activity in the UK, supplementing falling income from producing crops and animals. Today shooting can command £1,000 or more per day per gun. One consequence is that hunting can be severely restricted, especially during January. The reason put forward for restriction is that the presence of hounds, even a few days before a shoot, can disturb the birds and change their flight and, hence, the standard of shooting provided. Whether or not this is true, and the experience of the author casts doubt on this, if the paying guns believe this to be true, the owner of the shoot will insist that hunting does not take place in order to safeguard his shooting income.

In France, shooting for sport has developed in a much more individual way, mainly as a result of the laws on hunting stemming from the Revolution. It is sport practised every day throughout the country by men going out, often alone, with their dog or dogs. It is the sport sought by men who deliberately retire from the town to a small piece of land to practise it or they rent an area of forest. Particularly in the case of the latter, the dog they will use is a hound, often a basset. Their scenting abilities, voice and deliberate working habits are ideally suited for the purpose. This is probably the reason why the rough coated basset and the two more agile smooth coated breeds of basset, rather than the Basset Hound, are favoured.

The reputation of the basset for this type of shooting followed them when they were first imported into England in the latter half of the nineteenth century. As a result, many sportsmen did not, and many still do not, regard them as suitable for hunting as a pack because of their reputed temperament, relative speed and agility.

In about 1850 barbed and net wire, was introduced into England as a cheap means of enclosing land. This had considerable impact on the mounted packs and influenced the type of hound. In some areas it was so prevalent that riding was restricted. It also had effects on foot packs, especially the build of the hound. It may have been one of the reasons why the initial interest in bassets in the later part of the nineteenth century waned in the first half of the twentieth century. Anybody who has lifted bassets over net wire will testify to this! Wire is still not common in France.

Another reason for the initial success of the basset as a hunting hound in England may have been a result of the dissatisfaction with the beagle that had been developed by the first half of the nineteenth century. During that century the size of many packs had been reduced to 12in (31 cm), the so-called pocket beagle. These increasingly showed poor sport. By the end of the century the futility of this size of beagle was recognised and the modern beagle rapidly became the accepted norm, at the expense of the basset which was seen as too slow and more expensive to keep and to transport.

In the provinces of France, right through to the last King in the mid nineteenth century there was little interest in the Court other than by those living in or near Paris. Hunting in many forms was a common sport and food necessity for all classes of society. Each area tended to develop its own forms of hounds suited to the country and the quarry available. The large forests allowed stag and boar hunting with their attendant risks to remain the premier attractions for those that could afford the necessary hounds and horses. These were especially favoured by the Court circles around Paris who developed many of the rituals of vénerie. But the hare remained a firm favourite amongst most sections of the rural population, both mounted and on foot, because of the intricacies of its line.

All was ended in the First Revolution as all forms of hunting were banned. But this ban was overturned in the Second Revolution. That Constitution and the present Constitution enshrined the right of all to hunt on their own land and to follow the quarry on to the land of their neighbours. But the Revolution also put much of the land, especially the Forests, into the ownership of the State or the local Commune. That is still the position of much forest today. As a consequence, much hunting land has to be rented from the State or Commune, providing a useful income to them. The income generated from field sports is still a strong motivation in France for the retention of hunting.

The Napoleonic laws of inheritance have also had a great influence on land ownership. Under these laws, land inherited had to be equally divided between all children. As a consequence fields became fragmented. Poorer farmers not able to buy land to consolidate their holdings found themselves with small parcels of land, often separated from the other. This led to inefficient farming, poor yields and low income. The latter forced many of them to rely upon renting land from larger owners or selling their land and working as labourers.

Some of the consequences of these small land holdings, large forests and renting of hunting lands are that private packs tend to be small, family owned and run. The small number of hounds and land areas have tended to favour hunting to the gun, rather than 'en force'. These factors influence the type of hound.

Between 1875 and 1889 the disease phylloxera spread across France with disastrous consequences on the vine and wine production. Not only did this effect the vineyard owners, it badly effected the peasant population dependent upon it for employment and for their own wine. One result was a decrease in the number of hounds kept.

During the later part of the twentieth century regulation of hunting by the SCC and laws regarding kennelling and hunting have further restricted the size of many private packs. The SCC set up regional and local committees to oversee hunting throughout France. These determine the seasons for hunting, the number of days and the number of each quarry than can be killed. There is much emphasis on wild animal conservation. This, together with the traditions of 'vénerie', has led to the 'tally' being of lesser importance, with the greater emphasis on hound work, cry and breed conformation. So much so that some French hunting enthusiasts consider English hunting to be 'blood thirsty' because of the relatively high tally, especially with hare. This favours the basset.

Recent laws regarding kennelling have forced many owners to minimise the number of hounds in kennels and the number of whelps which they have. Many are now reliant upon professional breeders for their puppies. In 2002 a new law was introduced requiring every hunter, defined as anybody carrying a horn or a whip, to obtain an annual licence. This requires taking a theoretical examination on hounds, quarry and firearms and a practical firearms test. There is also a substantial annual fee.

The full effects of all this regulation have yet to be seen in France. There do seem to be moves towards the private packs being composed of smaller and slower breeds, including the bassets. There do seem to be moves away from hunting 'en force' to hunting with a gun, again favouring the basset. But there also seems to be a move towards greater interest in brevet de chasse – hunting trials. These are seen in France as having many advantages. The costs of renting a hunting area are shared. As killing the quarry is forbidden, more hunting hours can be obtained. Obtaining a brevet adds to the financial value of the hound. Buying and selling hounds is normal. Obtaining a brevet also allows owners to enter the working classes in dog shows, again enhancing the value of the hound and the reputation of the breeders. The brevet certainly goes a long way to countering the deficiencies of judging hounds in a show ring. Over a hundred of these one to three day events take place every year across the whole of France involving every type of foot hound on quarry from rabbit to boar. These are very convivial and family affairs.

In England, the Quarantine Laws of 1901 had a major impact on the basset in particular. Until that time the original stock and much of the replenishment of that limited stock was hugely dependent upon imports from Europe, particularly France. This ceased when the Laws came into effect, just at a time when the number of bassets in England had begun to decline. It was catastrophic because it led to considerable inbreeding and serious weakening in quality of the stock. This, in turn, led to out-crossing to revive the vigour.

In France, the problems for the basset were different. Bassets did not capture the imagination of French dog fanciers at the end of the nineteenth century as they did in

England. This may have been because there were far more types of hounds to choose from. The 1914–1918 War almost destroyed all bassets in France. After the War there was a shortage of hares most of them having been shot for food. Petit Vénerie turned to rabbits and small deer as substitutes. The then four major basset breeds, Artésien-Normand, Bleu de Gascogne, Vendéen and Bretagne had to be re-created almost from nothing. Their re-creation took note of the rabbit and small deer, as quarry and the use of the gun. Progress was slow and completely reversed with World War II, after which the bassets had almost disappeared once more and had to be re-created yet again. But this re-creation was in line with the Breed Standards now registered and overseen by the SCC. These Standards had seen increasing influence from show breeders. It was not until 1989 that the Basset Hound of England and the USA was recognised by the SCC as a breed distinct from the five recognised French basset breeds.

In recent years there have been yet more changes in land ownership and usage in the UK. State payment systems to farmers have favoured the development of the 'prairie' farm, particularly in East Anglia, with losses of hedges and verges, reduced crop diversity and much larger land holdings. Initially these appeared to cause a sharp decline in the hare population. But over the last ten years in particular hare numbers have increased substantially. However, over the same period the population of wild deer has rocketed. Whilst both bassets and beagles have benefited from the improvement in the hare population, the deer are now causing major problems. Large fields devoted to intensive grain production have benefited foot packs over mounted packs as a result of the damage that can be done by a large number of horses moving at speed.

In other parts of the UK, especially the Home Counties, the trend has been towards smaller land holdings, partly as result of the fashion to live in the country and commute to work. The consequent increases in the numbers of land owners and occupiers has vastly increased the time and effort which Masters have to spend in clearing land for hunting. Furthermore, the refusal of a single, sometimes small, land owner to allow hounds over or near the land held can result in the loss of a complete Meet. All over the UK huntable land is being constantly lost due to building of houses, factories, roads and airports. This is accelerating as agricultural prices decline and prices for development land increase. This is particularly true in the South East as a result of the shift of population. Further hazards have resulted from the electrification of much of the rail network. Foot packs have some advantage over mounted packs in these circumstances as less land is required to hunt. Bassets have a further advantage as, being slower than beagles, they can be controlled more easily.

Industrialisation of farming has had another detrimental effect on hunting. For much of the twentieth century there were sufficient people employed upon the typical farm to allow the farmer and/or his sons to take time off to hunt, often to serve as a Master or to hunt or whip-in to hounds. Increasingly this is no longer feasible. This has led to a shortage of people, especially the young, willing to take on these posts and a reduction of personal experience and knowledge of farming in hunts. The latter has been exaggerated by the influx of urban people able to use their cars to be active in hunting. This problem is more acute with foot packs than with mounted packs as the horse element attracts more women, a growing number of whom take on posts of Master and whips.

Whilst road and rail construction have also expanded in France, they do not yet significantly impact on hunting. France is, geographically, a much larger country than the UK. Although its population is higher, it has a much lower population density. Large cities are fewer and tend to be concentrated in the north, whilst much of the hunting is in the centre and south. Perhaps, more importantly, much hunting is in forests, not in open land suitable for development.

The shortage of young people coming into hunting is also being experienced in France, although not to the same extent as in the UK. France is experiencing a growth in older, retired men taking up hunting, often with their own small, private pack of hounds, quite frequently bassets or beagles. There has always been a wide appeal in France to retire to the country with a small amount of land. This is discussed more fully in the next section of this chapter. This may have been assisted by the high State retirement pensions.

Over the past two decades, there have been two major changes in mammalian wild life in France. The wild boar has now spread to almost every Department, often to levels threatening agricultural profit. There has been an increase in Hunts targeting the boar as their main quarry. Over the last five years, there has been a marked decline in the rabbit population, to the extent that they are now rare in Belgium and some of northern France. Since the end of WWI the rabbit has been the main, often the only, quarry for many packs of bassets. Some Hunts have switched to hare, sometimes with difficulty. The net results appear to be a decline in the use of Basset Hounds and of Basset Artésien-Normand and an increase in the rough coated bassets. One reason put forward is that the straighter legged bassets are more suitable for hare. But, in the author's opinion and experience, the main reason is that the show interests in these two breeds are now dominating the two Breed Clubs, to the detriment of hunting.

The Industrial Revolution and Industrialisation

The Industrial Revolution, beginning at the end of the eighteenth century, created a need to move raw materials to the factories and the new manufactured goods to the markets. It also resulted in increased movement of population from the country to the towns. None of these could be successfully accomplished without improvements in transport, especially the roads and the invention of the steam train.

John Loudon McAdam was born in Scotland, but made his fortune in New York before returning to Scotland in 1783, when he purchased an estate at Sauhrie in Ayrshire. There he noticed the poor state of the roads and set about finding ways of improving them by changing their profile and their construction. In 1798 he moved to Falmouth in Cornwall and continued his research. These ideas were refined during his appointment as Surveyor General of Bristol roads and resulted in what has become known as the macadam road, later improved by the use of tarmac. He finally became General Surveyor of Metropolitan Roads in Great Britain. This heralded a dramatic improvement in the roads in Great Britain and then in the United States and elsewhere.

George Stephenson was born in Wylam, Northumberland in 1781. In 1825 he built the first steam locomotive for hauling colliery wagons, followed in 1830 by the first public train, running between Darlington and Stockton. The latter led to the construction of the first inter-city railway between Liverpool and Manchester. By 1851 there were 6,800 miles of railway in the UK.

The small stocks of coal in France, largely restricted to the north, together with the much more rural population with fiercely independent regions meant that the Industrial Revolution occurred later and slower in France than in England. Even in 1913 industrial production in France was only forty-one million tons, compared to 292 million in Great Britain. This, in turn, restricted the development of transportation and had profound effects on the development of society in France compared to England. Hence a divergence in the styles of hunting and breeds of hounds. The late development of transport helped the regions of France retain their individual identities for much longer than in England, especially their predominantly rural, agrarian based structures. It has also resulted in urban life in France being concentrated in, relative to England, a few large cities, predominantly in the North. Even today, a higher proportion of the French population works or lives in the country or has close family ties to the land. The closer bonding of the family unit has also contributed to this affinity to the countryside.

In France, frictions between urban and the rural populations are less than in England. People tend not to live so much in each other's pockets. Urban life styles in France are different to those in England with a predominance of rented accommodation, rows of houses or flats, minimal gardens and high density. Land is not in such short supply as in England with much less jealousy over land ownership. Rural people are, on the whole, allowed to live their own way of life without undue pressures from 'in-comers'. Those that do retire to the country often do so because they want their own small piece of land to cultivate. These 'retirees' tend to adopt a rural style, not wanting to change rural ways to urban ways, as so often occurs in England.

Collecting and Fancying

Collecting plants and animals, especially those that were rare or exotic, has been a hobby from ancient times. But, until the eighteenth century it was largely the preserve of rulers and the wealthy. In the eighteenth century having a private collection became a signal to others of one's wealth and education. In 1765 the Imperial Menagerie at the Schønbrunn Palace in Vienna (established in 1752) was opened to the public and can be considered to be the first modern public zoo. The Jardin des Plantes was opened in 1793 in Paris and the Zoological Society of London at Regents Park started in 1828.

The new English moneyed classes of nineteenth century became avid collectors. Their fancies could be amply supplied with the improvements in sea transport, especially from the propeller-driven steamships, pioneered in 1843 by the *Great Britain* of Isambard Kingdom Brunel. At the same time the prosperity of that age allowed many people to become another form of collector, a fancier. Dogs were particularly popular and better transport allowed people to travel more readily, including to the Continent. Competitive showing of dogs started partly as a result of the banning of pit fighting. In 1834 Charles Aistrop, the landlord of the *Elephant and Castle* ale house in Westminster, organised a dog show for his customers and offered a silver cream jug as the prize. He continued these shows when he took on the *Eight Bells*. As a result of his shows he was elected Secretary of the Toy Spaniel Club. He was succeeded in this post by Charles Cruft. Cruft later went into partnership with James Spratt, who had produced one of the first dog biscuits. This gave Cruft access to the wealthy and influential. The first organised public dog show had been held in England at Newcastle-on-Tyne in 1859 and the first in London in 1861. Cruft got involved with the dog show at the 1878 Paris Exhibition. He then launched a terrier show at the Royal Aquarium and this led to Cruft's Great Dog Show in 1891, to which he persuaded Queen Victoria to exhibit her Pomeranians.

At the same time the rise in France in the early nineteenth century of pride in the Nation led to several movements to preserve and exhibit French culture in all its forms, including dogs. The Jardin d'Acclimatation was established in Paris in 1860 specifi-

The kennels of the Jardin d'Acclimatation in Paris, 1873.

cally to conserve French breeds of cattle and dogs. The first dog show in France took place in Paris in 1863 and included bassets.

Fairly rapidly prices for rare and exotic dogs rose, and the basset in England was initially considered to be one of these. High prices were, to some extent, encouraged by the practice of the show organiser requiring each exhibit to display a label showing the price asked for the dog. If the price was offered, the exhibitor had to sell. The organisers had a vested interest as they took forty per cent of the sale price. One result was that owners not wishing to sell a particular dog displayed a high price. This started at £100 to £200. But this proved to be too low. In 1900 Mr Arthur Croxton-Smith was exhibiting his basset Wantage. He did not want to sell it and displayed a price of £150. At one show his bluff was called when Mrs Tottie offered him the price. She, in turn, did not want to sell and, at the Birmingham National Show, made sure by exhibiting a price of £10,000 on five of her bassets!

On several occasions in England in the last three centuries fashions in dog fancying have been influenced by the choices of the Royal Family. The then Prince of Wales was given his first basset to mark the formation of the BHC in 1884 and became its first Patron. By the end of the decade he and his wife, the then Princess Alexandra, began to exhibit both smooth and rough haired bassets, including at Cruft's. This led to a surge in ownership of bassets. The royal couple continued showing bassets after they became King Edward VII and Queen Alexandra in 1901.

Ownership of dogs declined during the 1930s' recession and this decline was maintained during WWII. It was not until the economy revived in the 1950s that increasing dog ownership resumed. Soon the public were, once again, looking for novel breeds. The population by now was predominantly urban (less than five per cent working on the land) as increasing mechanisation of farming reduced the demand for farm labourers. The demand was for breeds that were perceived as requiring limited exercise and were fashionable. The Basset Hound was considered to be one of these, presumably on account of being low and, apparently, lethargic. The expanding economy resulted in greater advertising in the retail sector. One of the most influential campaigns was launched. This was for Hush Puppy shoes and featured a Basset Hound. This led to a boom in demand for them in the late 1950s and early 1960s. Their popularity and the efforts of Miss M.M. Keevil led to the formation of several packs based upon the Basset Hound, as distinct from the bassets derived from the pre-war Walhampton/Westerby breeding, later known as the English Basset.

As will be seen in the chapter on the History of Hunts, the gradual decline in the number of wealthy land owners from the late nineteenth century till today has had a profound effect on the ownership and organisation of basset packs in England, as it has with all the other forms of hunting. Initially, packs were private for the enjoyment of the owner and his friends and entirely paid for by the owner, referred to as the Master. The Kennel Huntsman and many of the Whips were waged, often working part time on the owners' estates. This way of life changed dramatically after the First World War. More and more packs were run by subscriptions from followers. This required the appointment of a Hunt Secretary, usually an Honorary position. By the 1930s, these subscriptions had to be augmented by the payment of a cap (or field money) by each person every time they followed the Hunt. At the same time the owner might appoint a Joint Master in return for a substantial annual donation to the running of the Hunt. These practices continued after World War II.

Labour costs and the accelerating break-up of the large estates as a result of death duty taxes further increased the problems of financing a Hunt. A growing number of Hunt Committees took on the task of raising money. Gradually they took responsibility for appointing Masters and ownership of hounds. One result has been a faster turnover of Masters and increasing numbers of Joint Masters. This has led to more frequent alterations in breeding policies and, to some extent, greater instability in type.

Hunting and Dog Associations

Foxhunting became the popular form of hunting at the turn of the nineteenth century in response to the desire for faster riding and more excitement. It was also used in the early days as a means of training racehorses and testing their speed and agility. Packs of foxhounds proliferated all over the country leading to bitter disputes over boundaries for hunting and for flesh. In 1856 a Foxhunting Committee was established at Boodles Club. Membership was restricted to a few wealthy members. It was primarily an elite dining club. In 1881 the MFHA was formed at Tattersalls.

In 1874 the Kennel Club was formed. It had two main functions – to regulate shows and to establish a Stud Book. To do the latter the Kennel Club also instituted written Standards for breeds which it recognised as 'pure bred'. Both were in response to the growing popularity of dog fancying and the rise of unscrupulous breeders and dealers, which was leading to a decline in the health of dogs. The idea of a Stud Book may also have been influenced by Darwin's works which had been published in the 1850s and 1860s. The concept of a 'pure breed' was, to some extent, a result of the new scientific ideas of classification. It also had its origins in family genealogy. But the main reasons may well have been a means of creating exclusivity and, in the case of the Kennel Club, control over Shows and a source of income (from registrations). In 1884 the BHC was formed for both rough and smooth coated bassets and was recognised by the Kennel Club. Masters became members, registered their hounds and showed at KC shows.

In contrast to these non-governmental bodies, in France the Société Centrale pour l'Amélioration des Races de Chiens en France was formed by the French Government in 1882. This was largely in response to the rise in interest in maintaining and promoting French culture. The prime objective was to preserve and improve the traditional French breeds of dog.Written standards and a stud book were instituted. In 1894 the Société de Vénerie was formed to protect and encourage hunting with hounds in France. These were later to become part of the SCC. This is still a Department of the Ministry of Agriculture and governs showing and all forms of hunting, including hunting trials (Brevet de Chasse). In 1896 the Club de Basset Français was formed covering both rough and smooth coated bassets and was recognised by the SCC.

In 1892, the AMHB was formed, along the same lines as the MFHA. Apart from settling disputes, a main pressure was to halt the decline in the quality of the beagle, especially the pocket beagle and the harrier. The AMHB established its own Stud Book and began to register countries. The latter was done in conjunction with the MFHA.

By the end of the nineteenth century disagreements began to surface between those hunting bassets and those who solely showed them. The disagreements centred on what was seen as the ill judged breeding of the show people with too great an emphasis on physical appearance, especially large heads, massive feet and pronounced crook. The former was a result of the view that the basset was descended from the Talbot and thus related to the Bloodhound. In addition, monetary considerations had begun to be a dominant influence in the breeding of dogs and in the management and policies of the breed clubs, including the BHC. Many Masters of bassets resigned from the BHC. In 1911 the MBHA was formed using the MFHA and the AMHB as models. A Stud Book was instituted but registration of countries was undertaken by the AMHB. Some Hunts also continued to register and show hounds with the Kennel Club. This continued until the reformation of the MBHA in 1958 when new rules were introduced banning the showing of hounds at KC shows.

These differences over breeding and commercial interests led to the downfall of the BHC. Public interest in the Basset Hound as a show dog rapidly declined and in 1921 the BHC had to be wound up, not to be revived until 1954. Between these dates the development of the basset was largely for hunting. As will be seen in chapters 6 and 7, it was from this stock that the post war Basset Hound was recreated.

In 1911 the FCI was formed, with France being a driving force. The FCI is an international umbrella organisation for national dog associations. It maintains international Breed Standards and organises shows and working trials, including hunting trials. Most countries are affiliated to the FCI. Whilst the Kennel Club is affiliated, the MFHA, AMHB and MBHA are not eligible as they do not recognise the FCI Breed Standards and maintain their own Stud Books.

The creations of the SCC and the FCI have been a major reason for the divergent developments of hunting in the UK and Europe. On the other hand, the separation of the Kennel Club and the MBHA from the SCC and FCI allowed the original Standards for the Basset Hound to be developed as they did. It was only the international power of the FCI that persuaded the Kennel Club to change the Standard for the Basset Hound to that of the US.

The differing operations of Stud Books of the KC and the Masters Associations have led to a divergence in the ways in which hound breeding for hunting has developed in England and in France. In France there is one Stud Book and one written Standard for each breed. There is no distinction between showing and hunting. A hound can only be entered in the Stud Book if both its parents are in the Stud Book. Furthermore, the Standards are now those of the FCI. This limits the ability of breeders to experiment with outcrosses and encourages in-breeding, with all its attendant problems. It places emphasis on visual appearance in a judging ring. Attempts have been made over the past few decades to modify this by the introduction of working classes with qualification through practical Brevet de Chasse. These favour movement, stamina and working qualities. However, the 'Beauté' classes are still seen by most breeders as more prestigious than the 'Travail' classes.

In England, the Kennel Club also maintains one Stud Book and one written Standard

PRICE 6D.

CATALOGUE

OF

Basset Hound Show

Promoted by *The County Gentleman & Land and Water*,

At Messrs. Tattersall's Yard, Rugby,

MAY 31ST, 1912.

The following Kennels exhibit :—

Lord North's.
Dallam Towers (Sir B. Wilson).
Dalby Hall (Capt. Burns Hartopp).
Greywell Hill (Hon. D. Carleton).
Walhampton (Capt. Heseltine).
Mr. Ivon Jones.
Riversfield (A. F. Towgood).

JUDGES :—

S. E. Owen Swaffield, Esq.
H. A. Bryden, Esq.
Otto Paget, Esq.

Judging will commence at 11 o'clock.

HON. SECRETARY—
HON. W. F. NORTH,
36-38, SOUTHAMPTON ST.,
STRAND. W.C.

Cover of the catalogue of the first show of the Masters of Basset Hounds Association held at Tattersall's Yard, Rugby on 31 May 1912.

for each breed it recognises. Bassets were included under Dachshunds or Foreign Dogs until 1876 as the basset was not recognised by the KC as a separate breed. However, the KC Standards are not always those of the FCI, although those for all basset breeds and for Beagles are those of the FCI. Again, a dog can not be entered into the Kennel Club Stud Book unless both its parents are registered in it. There are some exemptions to this rule but these are rarely allowed. The Kennel Club does not allow for or recognise any working trials or classes for hounds, although it does so for gun dogs and some other breeds, including Bloodhounds.

However, in contrast to France, the MFHA, AMHB and MBHA maintain their own Stud Books of hounds. All hounds accepted for registration have to have been entered to hunting in a recognised pack. There are no written Standards other than maximum heights. By means of Appendices to the Stud Books hounds resulting from an outcross of any nature can be put into the Appendix to the Stud Books. Progenies of Appendix hounds can get into the main Stud Book after a number of generations, specified by each Association. In the case of bassets, the MBHA allows any KC or FCI registered basset to go straight into the Stud Book. These procedures allow outcrossing without unduly encouraging it. The absence of written Standards allow hunts to develop their own type of hound to suit their country and the 'style' of the Hunt. This semi-open approach and absence of written Standards brings the benefits of out-crossing to long term vigour. A generalised Standard is maintained by encouraging hounds to be entered at Shows run by each of the Masters Associations by judges, an increasing number of whom have attended courses on judging. There is no aim to produce one type of hound or to produce only pure-bred hounds. But the number of Shows that can be entered each year is deliberately restricted. The rules of the Associations preclude showing of hunting hounds at KC Shows. The rules of the Associations also forbid members to sell hounds or to dispose of any hound except to another recognised pack.

As none of the hunting Associations are statuary bodies, unregistered packs of hounds do exist and are at liberty to acquire or dispose of hounds and to breed as they wish. They may or may not register hounds with the Kennel Club and may or may not maintain and publish their own Stud Books.

This divergence means that hounds can be imported into England and placed on a Stud Book of either the Kennel Club or a hunting Association. But it also means that English hounds only in the Stud Books of one of the hunting Associations can not be registered in France with the SCC and are unable to be shown or to be judged in most Brevet de Chasse or to be eligible to compete for the European Hunting Championships of the FCI. This restricts the use of English hunting bloodlines in Europe. With the small number of basset packs in England, this increases the problems of disposing of hounds.

On the whole, this 'open' nature of the Masters Associations Stud Books have worked to the advantage of working hound development in England. It has been of particular advantage to the basset as experience over more than a century has shown that outcrossing every ten to twenty years is necessary to maintain stock capable of hunting for sustained periods, showing good sport and retaining the essential characteristics of the bassets, especially cry. However the separation of hunting from showing in the UK does severely restrict the basset gene pool available to the relatively few basset packs in the UK. It also restricts the possibilities of rehoming bassets not required for hunting or when a hunt is disbanded.

Chapter Five

The Biological Origins of Bassets

To assist readers who may be apprehensive about wading through science, there is a summary at the end of this Chapter. The summary contains three highlighted words which can be used to refer back to an appropriate section in this Chapter. At the end of each section of this Chapter implications are drawn specific to bassets. It is hoped that this layout will allow every reader to derive some interest.

Breeding evidence

Early accounts of bassets, or any 'short legged' hounds, give little indication of how they were bred. Some literature suggests that the short legged puppies may have occurred in some litters naturally and not as a result of deliberate breeding. A well documented example is the cross which Monsieur Giet made in the 1880s which resulted in the sudden and apparently unexpected appearance of bassets which were then bred and became the foundation of the present Basset Bleu de Gascogne.

Dog fancying became popular throughout Europe in that period and breeders were looking for unusual types. In France La Jardin d'Acclimatation in Paris deliberately collected any type of dog, including bassets, which was considered to be a French breed.

Genetical evidence – Genetics

As we shall see later, spontaneous genetical mutations have been reported by medical and veterinary scientists. However the competitive nature of show breeders may never allow us to know the frequency of spontaneous occurrences of 'bassets' in litters. Breeders may wish to keep secret the source of their successes or, at least, to give the impression that the 'bassets' were a result of their expertise in breeding. Breeders of non-basset varieties probably put down any unexpected 'basset' forms and make no mention of them in order to preserve their reputation.

Many books published on bassets make no specific or detailed reference to the scientific basis of basset breeds. As with almost every breed, these books try to trace the breed back to Roman and Greek times, as though there was an unbroken history of deliberate selection. These books concentrate upon the recorded pedigrees. In the case of bassets, these can only be traced back with any degree of certainty to the nineteenth century. Veterinary research gives few clues as most of the work on dwarfism has been on dog breeds other than bassets. This is hardly surprising. Basset breeders expect and want bassets.

To find an origin for 'basset', a definition needs to be established. It is not sufficient to use the loose translation of the French 'bas' as 'low'. What is generally agreed is that a 'basset' is a short legged version of a hound. For example, in France the Griffon Vendéen come in four sizes: Grande, Briquet, Grand Basset and Petit Basset. The occurrence of the Briquet version shows how height alone is not sufficient to differentiate the basset. Similarly, there are three versions of the Bleu de Gascogne: Standard, Petit and Basset. There two versions of the Fauve de Bretagne: the Standard and the Basset.

The distinguishing characteristic of a basset is that the height is significantly less than the length of the back. It is a particular form of dwarfism. This is in sharp contrast to other hounds. In England one of the guidelines for judging hunting Foxhounds or Beagles is that they should fit into a square. That is to say that their height should be about the same as their length.Dwarfism is disproportionate. This can be contrasted with midget or miniature forms where the reduction in size is proportionate. An example is the Poodle. The distinction between proportionate and disproportionate (or primordial) dwarfism is made in the definitive book of 1993 on domestic animal pathology edited by Jubb, Kennedy and Palmer.

The definition of a basset breed adopted by the MBHA as a guide to judges includes the phrase; *'a hound with a height within sixty to eighty per cent of its length.'* The actual height is not needed in such a definition. Having a relatively long back will cause any hound to seem to be, comparatively, 'low' to the ground. This definition on its own could also encompass other breeds, in particular the Dachshunds. It is qualified by the MBHA as they will only register a basset in their Stud Book if at least one of the parents is registered either with them or with the Kennel Club as a recognised breed of basset.

Breeders and books on bassets have tended to avoid discussing scientific explanations of the origins of bassets, probably because these usually involve terms which are generally thought to be diseases and aberrations or are associated with disabilities. Research in this area is made more difficult by the fact that, until the 1970s, there was no generally accepted terminology. Even in the 1950s and 1960s, basset forms were referred to in veterinary terms as 'dwarfism', a term borrowed from the medical world who, sometimes, refer to 'the little people'. In 1969 a human classification was drawn up by the European Society for Paediatric Radiology of November, 1969. This classification is known as the Paris Nomenclature for Constitutional (Intrinsic) Disorders of the Bone. It was revised in May 1977.

Less research has been conducted in dogs than in humans, especially at the genetic and molecular levels. Assumptions are made that categories similar to those in Man occur in dogs; that the characteristics in dogs of each group are analogous to those in Man; and that the genetical causes are similar. These assumptions may not be entirely correct, but they do provide a useful model for the moment and will be used in this chapter. But readers should be aware that the rapid advances in genetics and molecular biology may give rise to different models in the foreseeable future. For example, the Human Genome project has now allowed us to be much more precise on genetical causes in man. The Human Genome Database lists 1,230 types of dwarfism and dysplasia, a generalised term for any abnormality of growth (from single cells to structures and complete beings). To date no equivalent detailed database has been constructed for any other mammal, although the Dog Genome Project is reaching completion. What is known is that over fifty per cent of the three hundred plus inherited canine diseases resemble specific diseases in Man.

A literature search shows veterinary research on forms of dysplasia relating to cows, goats, sheep, ponies and cats, as well as dogs. A more detailed search on dogs has revealed veterinary research on dysplasia (confined to leg length conditions) involving thirty-four different breeds (excluding varieties):

Alaskan Malamute	Australian Shepherd	Basset Hound
Beagle	Boston Terrier	Boxer
Bulldog	Chihuahua	Cocker Spaniel
Collie	Corlian Bear-dog	Dachshund
Dandie Dinmont	German Shepherd	Great Pyreneen
Irish Setter	Japanese Akita	Japanese Spaniel
Labrador	Norwegian Elkhound	Pekinese
Plott Hound	Pointer	Pomeranian
Poodle	Pug	Samoyed
Scottish Deerhound	Scottish Terrier	Shetland Sheepdog
Shizhtzo	Vizsla	Weimaraner
Welsh Corgi		

This veterinary research gives eighteen terms for identified causes for dysplasias of the limbs in dogs, plus the original umbrella condition of dwarfism. This list excludes lethal conditions which normally result in death at or soon after birth, including the most common human form of dwarfism, Thanatophoric dysplasia.

The most commonly reported forms in humans are in the groups Achondroplasia (ACH), Hypochondroplasia (HCH) and Pseudoachondroplasia (PCH). All are caused by genetical mutations. Molecular studies have shown that Multiple Epiphyseal Dysplasia (MED) is an allelic form of the same gene as Pseudoachondroplasia and is now included in this group. MED produces milder characteristics.

Whilst PCH is relatively common in humans, it is not reported very frequently in dogs, except in miniature poodles. It is unlikely to be the main cause of the bone conditions of bassets. Whilst it resembles the other two conditions, ACH and HCH, the effects are noticed as a puppy grows. Locomotion becomes progressively more difficult with the joints becoming enlarged and stiff. The shortness of the limbs becomes more and more obvious as the puppy grows. The limbs are often severely malformed. Ossification of the bone may be delayed and the cartilage structure is abnormal, giving a mushroom-like appearance. Osteoarthritis is commonly associated with the disease because the cartilage formed is more susceptible to wear than normal. The dwarfism probably occurs because of loss of growth plate chondrocytes as a result of the negative effects of the mutant gene.

Unlike the other two groups, in humans the condition can be genetically recessive, that is to say that it has to be inherited from both the father and the mother. It is autosomal, that is to say that the effected gene does not lie on the sex chromosome and is, therefore, not sexually linked in inheritance. The mutation is usually to the COMP gene (located at 19p13.1), occasionally to COL9A2 (located at 1p33-p32.2) or COL9A3 (located at 20q13.3). There are at least seventy known distinct mutations.

The most common, non lethal, cause of dwarfism in humans is ACH. Some 5,000 humans are estimated to have ACH in the USA and 65,000 worldwide. The occurrence is between 1 in 15,000 and 1 in 40,000 live births. Most infants with ACH are born unexpectedly to parents of average stature.

Unlike PCH, the effects of ACH in humans are evident at birth and are probably present in the foetus from an early stage. They are seen as abnormal growth of either bone or cartilage or both giving rise to shortened limbs or shortened trunk, a disproportionate dwarfing. The shortening of the limbs is often more pronounced in the upper part than the lower. In addition the skull is also effected, the mid-face being under developed and the forehead and jaw are predominant. The skull malformations can cause a narrowing of the spinal cord canal leading to pinching of nerves. This can result in difficulties in locomotion and poor control of the bladder and bowel.

In I.M. Oriol's work of 1986 and C.A. Francono's work of 2001, the gene mutation for ACH in humans is estimated to be between 1.72 and 5.57 x 10–5 per gamete per generation, which is high. The gene is located on chromosome 4 at G380R. It is thought to be the fibroblast growth factor receptor 3 (FGFR–3) gene. There are three other FGFR genes, none of which appear to be involved in this disease. The mutations have been found to be G1138A/C, substitution of an arginine residue for a glycerine residue at position 380 at nucleotide 1138. The FGFR–3 gene controls a very complex signalling system involving the production and use of fibroblast growth factor (FGF). The fibroblasts are responsible for the production of all forms of connective tissue. The effect of the mutation is thought to be by extending the length of inhabitation at the growth plates of the long bones giving a stunted growth. The terminal differentiation of the chondrocytes (the cartilage producing cells) is affected giving the characteristic thickening at the joints and, in some forms, the lax cartilages. It also alters the calcium matrix in bone and cartilage, weakening the matrices causing bending of the bone and enlarged and softer cartilage.

The gene was originally thought to be an autosomal recessive. In 2003, John Hopkins University classified it as an autosomal dominant. That is to say that it is not genetically linked to sex and need only be inherited from one parent.

Recent studies have shown that the mutation occurs much more frequently in the male than in the female, by a factor of about twenty-five. The reason for this is not fully understood. One reason may be that the production of an oocyte, female egg, requires cell divisions involving 23 chromosome replications, whilst the production of a male sperm involves 610 chromosome replications. As a mutation can occur during any chromosome replication, the male sperm has a twenty-five times greater chance than the female egg. Alternatively, if the mutation occurs early in the production of a germ-line, the mutation may be replicated in the remaining divisions, these being more in the male than in the female.

Studies have also indicated that the incidence rates of such mutations may increase with the age of the male. Again the cause is not known but may be associated with the fact that the number of cell divisions involved in the male germ-line increases with age, unlike the production of the female germ line.

The questions then arise as to how close the dog genome is to the human genome and to how close the genomes are between dog breeds. The answer to the latter is that about ninety-nine per cent of the genome sequences are identical between the four hundred or so dog breeds. Present indications are that dogs share about three quarters of the 2,900 gene sequences of Man. But dogs have thirty-nine pairs of chromosomes, compared to twenty-three in Man. Some of these additional pairs are associated with smell, a characteristic particularly well developed in scent hounds.

Using the human genome as a close model of the dog genome is also validated by the fact that dogs have more known inherited diseases than any animal, other than Man. Many of the 360 inherited dog diseases have human counterparts.

Several breeds of dog are thought to suffer from ACH, including Bulldogs, Boston terrier, Pug, Pekinese, Japanese spaniel and Shih Tzu. Some veterinarians also include the Basset Hound. However, the normal absence of any cranial deformities indicate that some other disease may be the prime cause. In the past veterinarians have tended to place the basset into the ACH group. As will be seen, this may not be correct.

The third group causing dwarfism in humans is HCH.This has many of the effects of ACH, but in less severe forms and without abnormalities to the cranium. HCH is not as common in humans as ACH. It has a much wider range and degree of effects than ACH. The cause is now known to be almost the same as ACH: a single, autosomal dominant mutant affecting the FGFR–3 gene. The difference is that the mutation is at base site 1620 rather than at 1138 and is labelled as C1620G/A. The rate of mutation for ACH is not yet known, but is probably less than that for ACH.

Many breeds of dog can exhibit abnormalities in the HCH group. These include Welsh corgi, Dandie Dinmont terrier, Scottish terrier, Skye terrier and Beagle. The Dachshund is sometimes included, but the common intervertebral disc disease and elbow abnormalities suggest that the Dachshund may not fit into the HCH group or indeed into any of the human categories.

HCH is now thought to be the predominant cause of the dwarfism exhibited by basset hounds. However it may not be the only cause. Literature suggests that more than one breeder was responsible for the modern forms of bassets. As dwarfism has been a characteristic which was deliberately encouraged, it is possible different breeders may have encouraged different forms. This possibility is made more plausible by the fact that many forms of chondroplasia occur spontaneously.

It is useful to compare the literature on bassets and the experiences of breeders with the known facts about HCH. A number of accounts from the nineteenth century indicate that a basset form arose in a particular litter more by chance than by design and that not all the litter were effected. In many cases, both parents appear to have been 'normal' dogs with no previous history of dwarfism. The example of the Basset Bleu de Gascogne was outlined in Chapter 3. The literature on other breeds suggests similar situations for the Basset Artésien and the Basset Vendéen. Literature on other breeds also suggests that many modern miniature varieties arose from the selection of unexpected small puppies. The same applies to miniature varieties of cats. All this accords with the known high rate of spontaneous mutation of the single gene responsible for HCH.

The Basset Bleu de Gascogne literature also indicates that it was the sire of the first examples who was responsible and that this dog was old. Both these observations accord with the research showing that the mutation rate is significantly greater in males and increases with age.

The literature frequently reports that breeding from a basset form almost always results in some or all of the litter being bassets. Similarly, the first generation of crosses between a basset and a non-basset are almost always reported as being all or mainly with basset characteristics. Both situations apply whether it is the sire or the dam which is a basset. This points to the source being non sex linked and genetically dominant, as is the case with HCH.

What we can conclude from this is that the most common physiological basis for 'bassetism' might be a genetical mutation in the chondroplasia group, possibly in the hypochondroplasia sub-group. It is highly likely that many different gene mutations will be found to be implicated. It is also possible that the different basset breeds may be found to be associated with different forms of chondroplasia and with mutations of different genes.

If hypochondroplasia is the prime cause in a breed, then it is likely that it is dominant and not sex linked. The implications of this are that 'bassetism' can be inherited from either the sire or the dam and that only one parent need be carrying the mutation. This would explain why most outcrosses to other non-basset breeds usually result in the whole of the first generation being bassets. What it also means is that other characteristics which are recessive may remain hidden for one or many generations. Hence the sudden re-appearance of long legs, rough or silky coats, curly sterns, unusual colourations, etc. It also means that undue use of non-basset blood lines, either directly as one of the parents or indirectly through past breeding, will result in an increasing number of whelps without any basset genetic mutation.

The physiological causes of 'bassetism' should be taken into consideration in rearing and looking after bassets. The main concern should be for the limb joints. As the bone matrix will be softer and weaker than in other breeds, the early feeding of the whelps is of crucial importance, particularly in ensuring that they receive sufficient calcium in a diet that has all the components necessary for the absorption and utilisation of calcium. In the early days this means paying very careful attention to the diet of the bitch. The problem is particularly acute with bassets as they tend to have large litters.

The enlarged and soft joints may also be accompanied by lax ligaments. Permanent damage can be done by allowing excessive exercise and by allowing puppies to jump from or to hard or high surfaces, including ground made hard by frost. Fortunately, unlike human beings, the calcification of the skeletal structures occurs is almost completed in the first six months. At the same time it is important to encourage muscle development to support the ligaments so as to avoid hypermobility. Monitoring weight is also important to ensure that the maturing joints are not being asked to carry excess weight. The dangers in the young hound are from knuckling over, excessive crook, feet being forced outwards, especially if this is uneven, and cow hocking. Not only will such malformations effect movement when adult, they will throw excessive loads on to the shoulders and the back, causing problems later in life. The abnormal limb joints are likely to produce arthritic conditions as they grow older. These are also likely to be problems with hounds that are worked too much or in hounds that are over weight.

Matters will be made worse if the top line is not fairly flat or if it slopes up or down unduly. Allied to this are problems resultant from a top line that curves away, often seen as a stern placed too low. Needless to say, the shoulders and the pelvis must be correctly angulated. Any one of these features will effect the pattern of locomotion and the loads sustained by the spine.

If the cause of bassetism differs between the various basic breeds of basset then this may have implications on cross breeding between basset breeds. As will be seen in Chapter 6, deliberate crosses between rough and smooth coated bassets have been tried in the UK: the Walhampton in the 1890s and early 1900s; the Castle Milk in the late 1940s; the West Lodge in the 1950s and the Black Mountain in 1998. Most of these have been found to be unsatisfactory.

The reasons given for failures of these smooth and rough crosses seem to revolve around the type of hunting which resulted. The Walhampton found rough coated hounds to be more like terriers than hounds. The West Lodge found them to be wayward, difficult to control and difficult to breed to a consistent type. The Black Mountain had similar experiences, including their tendency to fight in kennels. In all cases, the rough out cross was to Basset Griffon Vendéen. The smooth coated side were all of the Basset Artésien-Normand type with the exception of the Black Mountain which was Basset Bleu de Gascogne. What is not clear from these experiments is whether the unacceptable qualities arose from clashes related to the genetic causes of 'bassetism' or to clashes between characteristics of different types of basic hounds. We may have to wait for completion of the Dog Genome Project for an explanation.

Evolutionary processes

Remains at Boxgrove in Kent of 400,000 years ago suggest that Man may have eaten wolves, as well as keeping and training their puppies. Remains in Germany indicate that the wolf descendent had already undergone morphological changes by 14,000 years ago. Graves in Jordan and in Israel dated to 12,000 years ago contain puppies, although these may be tamed wolves rather than 'dogs'. True 'dogs' seem to occur from 10,000 years ago, one site being at Stone Carr in Yorkshire. By Roman times most of the main breed types had been developed. Formalisation of hound breeds for hunting and the rituals associated with hunting were developed in the Middle Ages. But it must be remembered that the grey wolf was common in medieval times and beyond.

There is no reason to believe that development of hounds only took place at one time. Using wolves in breeding dogs, especially for hunting, goes on even to modern times. During the reign of William the Conqueror (1066–1087) there were eight hundred parks, sixty-nine royal forests and thirteen chases established for hunting in England. Certainly, specialist hounds were developed to hunt wolves in the medieval times, one being the Talbot, possibly descended from the St Hubert. These hounds would have been relatively slow and a basset would not have been out of place. It was not until James I (1603–1625) that a faster style of hunting became fashionable in England and hounds bred accordingly. As the wolf died out and the laws on hunting declined, foxhunting became more popular, to the extent that, by the end of the eighteenth century, the old, slow, Southern hound had all but died out. With it may have gone what bassets there had been.

The morphological changes from wolf to dog are thought to be consequences of 'ownership' by Man. 'Ownership' is likely to have been by restraint (isolating, tying up and generally controlling their movement) and would include trading them. It is thought that the selection processes may have looked for docility, lack of fear and stress tolerance as well as for their hunting, retrieving or guarding abilities. The former qualities may have been associated with hormonal changes, bringing about a reduction in brain size, less acute hearing and retention of juvenile characteristics and behaviour into adult life.

Hemer, in his 1990 book, points out that coat colour can be associated with temperament. Small, pale coated dogs may have been more manageable. Droop ears, reduced hearing and curled tails all reduce communication amongst a pack of dogs, making them more dependent upon their owner. Heavy coat curtails speed and hair over the eyes impedes vision. Small size may have originally occurred from poor feeding, along with restricted living conditions. This led to preferences for smaller size with associated mutations, including those effecting reproductive capacity and large litters and with shorter life spans. Shorter and wider muzzles may have led to a reduction in tooth size as a result of overcrowding. 'Stop' resulted from changes in curvature and the angles of a shortened mandible, with greater rounding of the eyes and more forehead with swollen frontal sinuses. Many of these characteristics typify the basset.

The primary features distinguishing the dog from the wolf are trainability and tameability. None of the wild canids exhibit either of these. This is thought to be because wolves lack the associated motor genetic sequence which other dogs have. Three theories have been put forward as to how these differences came about:

1 By selection trait by trait
2 By a process known as neoteny
3 By hybridisation.

Trait Selection

The assumption is that traits were deliberately selected and bred for. In the case of hounds, it was improved hunting abilities. There may have been other traits. One example is short legs. These may have been an unintended outcome associated with some other trait. Some limited research indicates that many hunting traits are genetically inherited. There is some evidence in foxhounds that giving tongue on a line is genetically dominant over muteness. In the case of bassets, the selected trait might have been deep scenting and this may be associated with the genetical set related to scenting ability. Such accidental traits may have been reinforced by further selection. Traits are usually not due to a single genetic group and are not independent of other traits. The selection of one may alter others. For example, silver foxes bred for docility also develop morphological changes altering the position of the tail, dropping of the ears, coats which are black and white piebald and alterations in their breeding pattern. Selections would have been made for behaviour and physical construction, not for what the dog looked like. Coat colour, for example, need not be genetical. A dog is white because it lacks melanin pigment. This is associated with derivates of tyrosine, including adrenalin and dopamine. Both these are associated with trainability. So that the great white hounds of France may have been originally developed for their trainability. Their white colour later became synonymous with a biddable hound. But as W.E. Beamis commented in 1984: '*When considering the diversity of dog breeds, it is unreasonable to propose rational adaptive explanations to account for each of these changes . . . Rather, some, perhaps most of the changes are interpreted as the product of selection operating on a restricted set of characters.*'

Research on heritable traits is very difficult to interpret. It is fairly clear that results may be specific to breed and age. Bearing all this in mind, one study by Greiger in 1972 is of interest as it bears out accepted practices in hunting packs that the bitch is more important than the dog. The study was on German Wire Haired Pointers. One table in this relates to scores calculated for the degree, one could say probability, which the dog or the bitch passes on specific traits to their offspring, 1.00 being 'always' and 0.00 being 'never'.

Trait	Sire	Dam
Hare tracking	0.03	0.46
Nose	0.01	0.39
Obedience	0.01	0.19
Seek	0.00	0.41

(Greiger, G. 1972. P. 55, Table 4.6.)

A further study was published in 1998 by Schmutz and Schmutz using 484 dogs of five breeds of dogs: German Short and Wire Haired Pointers, Griffon, Large Munsterlander and Poodle. It is of interest as it indicates how breeds have developed with the ability to pass on required characteristics. It also indicated that there were differences between short haired and wire haired breeds. They looked at the probability for the inheritance of seven traits: scenting, searching, retrieving (in water), pointing, tracking, desire to work and co-operation. They found a wide variation between breeds. The German Short Haired Pointers had probabilities of between 0.3 and 0.5 for scent, search, retrieve, track and work, whilst the Wire Haired had probabilities of about 0.3 for search and co-operation. On the whole the Griffons had low probabilities, except for scent. Similarly for the Munsterlander with high probability for only pointing. The Poodle had mainly low probabilities, with the exception of retrieving.

Neoteny

This theory was advanced by Raymond Coppinger and Richard Schneider in James Serpell's 1995 book. They suggest that the selection processes in deriving dogs from wolves may have been for juvenile behaviour, not for their working abilities. Some neonatal characteristics continue through adolescence and remain in the adult form. Normally juvenile behaviour changes during adolescence and is replaced in the adult. Coppinger and Schneider cite that a neonatal can not chew and an adult can not suck. Yet an adolescent can do both. They point out that most mammalian juveniles can play and learn better than adults. Play is a mixture of mainly non-functional neonatal and adult behaviours. Learning requires the physical patterning of motor neurons. They suggest that all domesticated animals exhibit some degree of neonatal patterns in the adult. Examples in dogs are begging for food, chasing a ball, sitting, etc. Under this theory, hounds would have been selected because of their retained juvenile characteristics of submission, docility and ability to learn. In the case of the basset, added to these may be their retention into adulthood of 'baby like' characteristics of large heads, large and open eyes and size.

Hybridisation

The third theory is that the development occurred through hybridisation as a result of cross breeding. Cross breeding can result in physical and behavioural changes to accommodate major differences between the parents. In the case of the basset, these could be the large chest to accommodate the lung and heart capacity needed for the bulk and for the crooked legs required to accommodate this large chest. However, in the case of dogs, most cross breeding occurred relatively recently, especially during the nineteenth century.

The probability is that all three processes have been involved. In the case of hounds, in particular the basset, neoteny may possibly have played a larger part than in other breeds. This could be especially true if one of the early reasons for keeping wolf like animals was for puppies to be companions to children. Certainly, placement of dogs in the graves of young children is a very old custom.

Evolutionary times

The generally accepted view is that the grey wolf, *Canis lupus,* is the only, or at least the principal ancestor of the dog. This is based upon behaviour, vocalisation, morphology and molecular biology. It is also of interest that most types of dogs appear to have originated in the Northern hemisphere in which there were the main communities of the grey wolf. There was a sub-species of the grey wolf, *Canis lupus Pallides.* This occurred in the Arabian peninsular, through Iraq and Iran to Pakistan. By some, this is thought to have been the most likely ancestor of the hound.

Current research strongly indicates that the development took place in a number of areas at a number of different times. It was not a unique occurrence that spread throughout the world. In her paper at the 2004 meeting of the American Association for the Advancement of Science in Seattle, Dr Deborah Lynch suggested that there may have been as many as ten occurrences. Each occurrence led to a separate group of dogs. The oldest may have been the gazehound of the Middle East, 8,000 years ago. This resulted in the modern day Greyhounds, Afghan and Pharoah Hounds.

The scent hounds have recently been shown to be a separate genetical group from the gazehounds, although Dr Lynch followed the traditional thinking that they may have evolved from the gazehounds. Also in Egypt, a group of toy and companion dogs seem to have arisen, the progenitors of our present day Maltese. In the Stone Age, the guard, herding and working group seem to have arisen in Tibet, the ancestors of our Mastiffs. Another group are the Northern hounds, such as the Elkhound, adapted to colder climates. The Pointer group also appears to be ancient. The Flushing Spaniel group may have arisen from dogs selected by tribes in Romano Britain, whilst the herding group may have been developed by the early Celts, who brought them to Wales. A separate group may be the Water Spaniel/Retriever group, possibly descendents of the original Irish Water Spaniel and Newfoundland. The tenth group are the Terriers.

These different occurrences have led to the enormous variation of dog that we have today from the miniatures to the mastiffs. There are more variations in breed in the dog than there are in any other domesticated species.

The interest in this theory for bassets is the suggestion that the rough haired and smooth haired bassets may have come from two different groups. The smooth haired almost certainly came from the Northern Scenthound group. However, the rough haired almost certainly originated in Brittany, the home of the Celts. The Celts are associated with both the Herding and the Terrier groups. If the ancestors of the two groups of basset are different, it is possible that they have differing genetic make-ups. Some negative consequences of cross breeding were referred to earlier in this chapter.

However, research published in 2000 on the dog genome by Dr Elaine Ostrander at the Fred Hutchinson Cancer Centre in the USA has indicated that there are four genetic groups of dog:

1 An ancient group originating in Asia and Africa. Includes the Alaskan Malamute and Siberian Husky. Thought to be the closest relation of the wolf.
2 The Mastiff group.
3 The Herding group, which includes Shetland and Belgian sheepdogs and Collies.
4 The Hunting group.

The research indicates that most breeds in the last three groups are of, comparatively, modern origin, possibly during the last two to three hundred years. The research was conducted using material from only 414 dogs from eighty-five KC breeds, out of over four hundred known breeds. This relatively small sample of individual dogs and of breeds may account for only four groups being found, compared to the ten suggested by Dr Deborah Lynch. If this theory is correct, then the traditional assertions are incorrect that modern hounds, including bassets, date back to Norman, Greek or even Egyptian times. Hunters in medieval and older times may have used hounds developed from the first and second groups. The classical St Hubert hound might have been from the Mastiff group.

Summary

Bassets are distinguished by having **genetical** mutations leading to shortening of the limbs. The most likely cause is in the group known in humans as hypochondroplasia. The biochemical and physiological results of hypochondroplasia have particular implications in breeding and in the early life of bassets. The evolution of the dog from the wolf probably involved more than one process from three possible **processes**: trait selection, neoteny and hybridisation. All three processes have implications in the breeding and welfare of bassets. Dogs evolved from the grey wolf at several different **times** in several different areas of the world. It is possible that the bassets are descended from more than one of these groups and, consequentially, may have different genetical profiles.

Chapter Six

Basset Packs of England, Scotland, Wales and Ireland

A wide definition of 'hunting' has been taken. Gun packs have not been included with one exception: the Sandringham as they were registered with the MBHA to allow their Majesties to show at the MBHA events. They were never hunted.

Ninety packs of bassets are known to have hunted in Great Britain and Ireland since 1872 (excluding the Sandringham). Almost half only existed for five or fewer years. But most of these existed in the late nineteenth century. The record for the longest activity, sixty-four years, is held by the Westerby.

There have been two periods of maximum activity. Between the 1890s and the 1910s, there were between sixteen and twenty-three Hunts active in each decade. Between the 1960s and the 1970s, there were between seventeen and twenty-one Hunts active in each of the respective decades. In current decade (2000s) there have been fourteen Hunts.

Before WWII, most of the Hunts were private with hounds often owned by a single Master and kennelled at his expense. The Master usually hunted the hounds and his estate staff looked after them in kennels and whipped-in, that is he assisted the Huntsman control hounds in the field. Hunting was at the convenience of the Master and following was by his invitation. Capping, that is a small payment by each follower on the day (put into a cap held out at the beginning of the day), was started in the 1900s by a few Hunts at the rate of 2s. 6d. (12½ p). Annual subscriptions started about the same time, usually one or two guineas (£1.05 or £2.10).

After WWII, more and more packs became the property of Committees, who also appointed the Masters. Both hunting and whipping-in became posts offered to amateurs, unpaid, members, rather than paid staff, originally known as Hunt Servants, now Hunt Staff. The subscription rates and caps rose very little until the late 1960s. Since then, they have tended to double every decade and are now about £120 for a single subscription and £5 a day for a cap. The increases in subscriptions and cap have resulted from the escalating costs of keeping hounds, especially as the majority of basset packs are now at livery with a pack of other hounds. In addition, transport and insurance costs have constantly risen.

The development from a single Master, privately owned pack to Committee managed pack has had other effects. The tenure of Masters has decreased and the number of Joint Masters have increased. This, in turn, has had effects on hound breeding as this is usually the responsibility of one of the Masters. The higher turnover of Masters has tended towards more frequent changes in breeding policies.

The following Table shows the county in which each Hunt has mainly been associated. At the end of this Chapter there is a Table by Hunt recording the known Masters and their tenures.

TABLE OF HUNTS BY MAIN COUNTY

LOCATION	COUNTRY	PERIOD	PAGE
Bedfordshire	Wrest Park	1924–25	**72**
Berkshire	Walhampton	1918–20	**58**
Berkshire	Grims	1951–64	**78**
Berkshire	Test Valley	1970–75	**96**
Berwickshire	Stainrigg	1902–11	**64**
Buckinghamshire	Mursley	1908–10	**69**
Buckinghamshire	Mr Jocelyn Lucas's	1914–15	**82**
Buckinghamshire	Sir Jocelyn Lucas's	1955–58	**82**
Cambridgeshire	Easthampstead	1881–93	**55**
Cambridgeshire	Mr M B Kennedy's	1881–87	**54**
Cambridgeshire	Walhampton	1891–93	**58**
Cheshire	Melancthon	1968-02	**93**
Co. Down	Moyola Park	1898–99	**63**
Co. Down	Mid-Down	1968–72	**94**
Co. Kildare	BHC of Ireland	1966–89	**89**
Co. Leix	Maj. Kemmis's	1903-04	**65**
Co. Meath	Slane	1903–10	**65**
Co. Westmeath	Mr Baylay's	1903-04	**65**
Devon	Stoodleigh	1900-01	**64**
Devon	Crowcombe	1951–65	**81**
Devon	Crealy	1977–89	**102**
Devon	Stevenstone	1968–72	**73**
Dorset	Iwerne Minster	1913–17	**70**
Dorset	Tank Corps	1919–23	**71**
Dorset	Huckworthy	1969-04	**95**
Dumfriesshire	Castle Milk	1938–62	**75**
Dumfriesshire	Craigcleuch	1959–68	**84**
Essex	Walhampton	1910–14	**58**
Essex	De Burgh	1960-	**85**
Fifeshire	Walhampton	1916–18	**58**
Fifeshire	Dalby Hall	1917–19	**66**
Glamorgan	South Wales	1966–98	**90**
Glamorgan	Black Mountain	1998-	**103**
Gloucestershire	Wick & District	1924–36	**72**
Gloucestershire	Miss Ena Adam's	1926–27	**71**
Gloucestershire	Dalby Hall	1928–31	**66**
Gloucestershire	Eastington Park	1928–40	**73**
Gloucestershire	Leadon Vale	1967-	**91**
Gloucestershire	Bradley Vale	1974–81	**99**
Gwent	Lord Tredegar's	1914–33	**70**
Gwneydd	Mr A-D-Smith's	1896–97	**63**
Hampshire	Danebury	1885–90	**57**
Hampshire	Wintershill	1889–98	**57**
Hampshire	Walhampton	1890-03	**58**
Hampshire	Wolvercote	1895–96	**62**
Hampshire	Greywell Hill	1902–14	**65**
Hampshire	Westerby	1939–40	**73**
Hampshire	Test Valley	1969–72	**96**
Herefordshire	Herefordshire	1958–66	**84**
Herefordshire	Ryeford Chase	1981-	**99**
Hertfordshire	West Lodge	1950-	**76**
Highland	Argyll & S. High.	1912–13	**64**

LOCATION	COUNTRY	PERIOD	PAGE
Huntingdonshire	Riversfield	1903–13	**65**
Kent	Sitka	1902-08	**66**
Kent	Chiddingstone	1897-03	**63**
Kent	Knowlton	1900	**64**
Kent	Fairforth	1909–16	**69**
Kent	Royal Tank Corps	1923–26	**71**
Kent?	Waltham	1933–37	**73**
Kent	Ringwould	1961–64	**87**
Lancashire	Mr Woodhouse's	1884–90	**56**
Lancashire	Riversdale	1886–90	**57**
Lancashire	North Lancashire	1907–11	**66**
Leicestershire	Dalby Hall	1906–25	**66**
Leicestershire	Walhampton	1920–33	**58**
Leicestershire	Westerby	1933–39	**73**
Leicestershire	Scalford Hall	1940–54	**76**
Leicestershire	Westerby	1947-	**73**
Lincolnshire	Reepham	1902-03	**64**
Lincolnshire	Casewick	1948–50	**81**
Lincolnshire	Test Valley	1972–75	**96**
Lincolnshire	East Lincolnshire	1975-	**100**
Norfolk	Brancaster	1927–33	**71**
Norfolk	Rallye Beauvautrait	1996-04	**102**
Northamptonshire	Polebrooke	1893–96	**61**
Northamptonshire	Delapré	1894-04	**62**
Northamptonshire	Westerby	1940–47	**73**
Northumberland	Mr Letts's	1998-04	**103**
Not known	Dale Park	1888–93	**57**
Not known	Mr Vincent Eyre's	1900-01	**64**
Not known	Street Ashton	1902	**64**
Not known	Maj. Wilkie's	1928–29	**72**
Not known	Capt. R Law's	1935–39	**75**
Not known	Mr Mellor's	1938–39	**75**
Nottinghamshire	Miss Barlow's	1937–38	**75**
Oxfordshire	Wroxton	1907–33	**67**
Oxfordshire	Mr V Fleming's	1911–15	**70**
Oxfordshire	Fourshires	1963-	**88**
Perthshire	Kilspindie	1956–69	**84**
Powys	Petre Uchaf	1973–82	**94**
Powys	Hyndfar	1982–84	**94**
Ross-shire	Ross-shire	1972–73	**94**
Rutland	Col. Reynardson's	1900-01	**64**
Rutland	Albany	1972-	**97**
Shropshire	Morfe Valley	2001-	**103**
Staffordshire	Dalby Hall	1926–27	**66**
Suffolk	East Suffolk	1961–67	**87**
Surrey	Lord Onslow's	1872–84	**52**
Surrey?	Buckland	1908–12	**69**
Sussex	Brighton	1887	**57**
Sussex?	Cookridge	1893–97	**62**
Sussex	Burgonet	1958–75	**84**
Warwickshire	Mr V Eyre's	C. 1900	**64**
Warwickshire	N. Warwickshire	1955–65	**83**
Warwickshire	Oaston	1962–75	**87**

LOCATION	COUNTRY	PERIOD	PAGE
Westmoreland	Dallam Tower	1898–14	**63**
Wiltshire	Highworth	1896-00	**63**
Yorkshire	Wheatley Park	1894–99	**62**
Yorkshire	Miss Ena Adam's	1923–26	**71**
Did not hunt	Sandringham	1877–22	**53**
By invitation	BHC (first)	1883–85	**55**
By invitation	BHC (second)	1955–72	**82**

BHC = Basset Hound Club

Each Hunt is now covered in the chronological order of its formation as a pack. An asterisk indicates MBHA recognition.

Lord Onslow's (1872–1884)

In 1871, as a young man, the 4th Earl of Onslow inherited considerable estates in north-west Surrey and in Essex with debts; a large Palladian house at Clandon, near Guildford, Surrey, set in an extensive deer park. The farming recession of the 1870s created further financial strains, requiring a mortgage of £1 million to be taken out. The Earl was descended from two Speakers of the House of Commons and held a number of Government posts. The Earl and Countess undertook the usual grand tour of Europe. More and more the couple lived in London for Society and for Government duties. Clandon was their country seat for entertaining and country sports. In 1888 they left England for New Zealand, the Earl having been appointed Governor General. This post involved him in further expense.

Lord Onslow initially had Dachshunds, these being popular after Queen Victoria received some as a wedding present from friends of the Prince Consort. Lord Onslow exhibited Waldman at the Crystal Palace Show in 1871. In 1877 Lord Onslow had a Dachshund bitch which he sent to the Rev. George Charles Lovell of St Edmund's Hall, Oxford, presumably for mating as the bitch was returned to the Earl by Lovell. Mr Lovell was a Committee member of the Kennel Club and a frequent judge.

Through the Dachshund connection, Lord Onslow may have become more acquainted with Lord Galway. In 1872 Lord Onslow acquired the entire kennel of bassets of Lord Galway. He bred from Basset and Belle and then, through Everett Millais, imported from France four hounds from the Comte de Couteulx in 1874. Most of his hounds. carried the characteristics of the original hounds: *shorter ear leather, high rears, and downhill top lines.*

Lord Onslow's main interest in the bassets was probably showing, although they were also used for hunting. In a letter written in March, 1879 to his Clandon Agent, Bowles, he says: *'I think the Bassets hunted through the coverts the previous day would drive the hares out & a few carrots thrown down the last day or two of this week is sure to draw them into the pack. I imagine that if the frost lasts the dogs will not be able to hunt.'* Again in November 1879 he says: *'You are welcome to have the Bassets at any time & to go any where. I am only too glad to get them hunted.'* In 1880, a Mr Peake wrote *'They are the admiration of everyone who sees them and they have hunted with my beagles very well.'* Two of the hounds involved were Tacitus and Trojan.

By this time bassets were attracting a lot of attention as curiosities in the dog fancying and show world. At that time, dogs were put up for sale at shows. Bassets were beginning to fetch high prices. Lord Onslow was asking between five to seven guineas.

In correspondence of 1881 Mr Krehl is to be offered three hounds at eight to ten guineas. The 5th Earl later stated that the 4th Earl had fourteen to fifteen couple of bassets in kennel in 1882. In June 1881 a letter suggests that all the bassets and puppies had been sold to Mr Krehl. However the entire sale may not have gone through as, in December 1883, Lord Onslow offers Mr F. Edwards of Southampton three mature and two young hounds at between four and ten guineas. In February 1884 he is offering to sell Juno and two puppies whelped in 1882 by Proctor at eight guineas for Juno, five guineas for the dog puppy and four guineas for the bitch puppy. He also wrote to Mr H.E. Sugden of Ashby-de-la-Zouche, Leicestershire; Mr H.A. Watson of Jesus College, Cambridge; Mr N.B. Shepard of Northampton (he was the Secretary of the new Basset Hound Club) and Mr R. Cadman of Malton, Yorkshire. In a letters of February 1884 it would appear that Mr Watson of Jesus College, Cambridge purchased Juno at five guineas and a bitch puppy at four guineas. Messrs. Krehl and Millais may have purchased the remainder. The Earl was one of the first members of the Basset Hound Club (BHC) in 1884.

The kennels for the bassets were at Merrow. The last kennelman was Mr T. Pick, who took up the post when he retired as butler to Lord Onslow. Before he disposed of all his bassets, Lord Onslow gave some to Mr Pick. One of these was Queen Dido'82 (14307). Mr Pick later bred, showed and sold bassets. Mr and Mrs Pick left the kennels in about 1887 and settled in Guildford. They continued to breed and sell bassets. The kennels remained standing until the 1980s when they were pulled down.

Thus, Lord Onslow's hounds were the first modern bassets to be hunting as a pack on hare in England. The Earl and his pack were instrumental in establishing the basset as a hunting hound and did much to popularise it in the show ring. His association with Sir Everett Millais eventually led to the creation in England of a new breed, the Basset Hound, with the involvement of George Krehl.

** Sandringham (1884–1922)*

From at least 1876 the Prince of Wales, later King Edward VII, kept dogs at Sandringham, which had been purchased by his mother, Queen Victoria, in 1870. In 1879 Queen Victoria had kennels built in Home Park, Windsor. In 1903 King Edward VII closed the Windsor kennels and transferred all the dogs to the kennels he already had at Sandringham. In 1936, the Sandringham kennels were closed by King Edward VIII. They were re-established at Sandringham by George VI and exist to this day.

It is known that the Prince of Wales owned and showed Dachshunds in 1876. The first he owned may have been Moscow (7855) who was exhibited in 1877. It is not known if it was smooth or rough haired. It was probably presented to him by Mr Routonzan Tolstoy and may have been descended from Russian stock.

Following the formation of the Basset Hound Club of Great Britain in 1884 and seeking Royal sponsorship, Mr George Krehl presented the Prince of Wales with a couple of smooth haired bassets. Both of these had been sired by the Comte le Couteulx's Ch. Jupiter. Apparently the Prince was taken by the *'quaintness'* of the hounds and showed his delight by presenting Mr Krehl with a scarf pin in the design of the Prince's Plumes.

In about 1890 further bassets were added to the Sandringham kennels: Babil (30429) and Bijou. These were both rough coated bassets. They were presented to the Prince by the Comtesse de Paris. The Comtesse was the wife of the claimant to the French throne and bred bassets at Stowe in Buckinghamshire. Her stock may have originated from Profiterolles (32942), which had been imported by Mr Tom (Ruck) Keene of 11 Queen's Gate, London from the Comte de Marois.

Queen Alexandra at her Sandringham kennels with rough and smooth coated bassets.

The Prince entered four rough haired bassets, which he had bred, at the first Cruft's in 1889 at the Royal Aquarium. This Royal patronage of both the breed and of the Show guaranteed success to both the breed and the show. The Prince became the first Patron of the Kennel Club when it was formed in 1891.

King Edward VII and Queen Alexandra continued to breed both rough and smooth haired bassets at Sandringham. Their interest was purely in showing, the pack being the only pack allowed to register with the MBHA who did not actively hunt. Indeed, it is known that Queen Alexandra would not allow shooting near the gardens at Sandringham and was opposed to foxhunting.

When King Edward VII died in 1910 Queen Alexandra continued her interest in the bassets at Sandringham. But, after the Great War the popularity of bassets declined and the number of opportunities diminished to show in a breed class for bassets. After 1922 her interest in bassets ceased and no more were bred at Sandringham. Queen Alexandra died at Sandringham in 1925 and this ended the Royal family's interest in the breed. The Sandringham blood was used extensively by the Walhampton through their use in 1911 and 1912 of Sandringham Zero'09 (373Q), a smooth coated, tricolour dog.

** Mr M.B. Kennedy's (1881–1887)*

Mr Miles (or Myles) B. Kennedy was a Master of his own pack from 1881 to 1887, hunting near Cambridge. He showed hounds and was one of the early members of the Basset Hound Club formed in 1884.

He may have acquired one of his first bassets from Everett Millais: Oscar (14306) (also known as Hector). In 1881 he used the imported bitch, Mignarde, from France which was put to the famous import of 1880 Fino de Paris (11060), owned by Mr Krehl and Mr Clement. The result was Finette '81. He put this bitch to another 1880 import owned by Mr Krehl and Mr Clement, Jupiter (12153) and produced Julie '84 (16717). He also used Fino de Paris twice in 1883 to produce a litter by Mr Krehl and Mr Clements's 1880 import of Comte de Couteulx's Guinevere (12148) and another by Lord Onslow's import Juno. In about 1883 he acquired at least four hounds from Mr T. Pick: Violet, Jealousy (13852), Queen Dido (14307) and Fanchette (16948). Mr Pick had been the Kennel Man for Lord Onslow. Only one of these hounds, the bitch

Fanchette '83, seems to have been used, producing Easthampstead Bachelor '85. But no use seems to have been made of this latter hound.

Mr Kennedy had many successes in the show ring as well as hunting one of the early packs of bassets in England on the hare. His pack seems to have been disposed of in about 1887 and there are no records of where the hounds went.

** Easthampstead (1881–1893) (Mr A.C.C. Kenyon Fuller's)*

Owned Mr A.C.C. Kenyon Fuller of Knebworth, Hertfordshire and also of Finchampstead, , Berkshire. He was a supporter of the Show hound and, as such, the majority of his breeding seems to have been based on that of other Show breeders, rather than active hunting packs. In a letter of about 1903 to Bryden, the author, Godfrey Heseltine said: *'I believe Major Croker and Mr Miles B. Kennedy were two of the first ever to attempt hunting a hare with basset hounds, about 1886.'* Major Croker had the Brighton Bassets.

Mr Fuller's first hound was Bachelor, by Jupiter (12152) out of Miles Kennedy's Fanchette (16948). Jupiter had been imported by George Krehl from the Jardin d'Acclimatation in Paris , where he was known as Bosquet and was a tricolour Champion hound, bred by the Comte le Couteulx in 1878. Some of his hounds were used by active packs, especially the Cookridge and the Polebrooke, and, to a lesser extent, the Delapré, the Wheatley Park and the Walhampton.

Easthampstead in kennels.

The Basset Hound Club Pack (1883–1885)

The Basset Hound Club was formally created in 1884. But on Friday 28 December 1883 the first meet of the embryo Club took place at the home of Mr H. Wyndham-Carter at Kennington, Kent with the objective *'to encourage the breeding of these handsome hounds'.* The pack consisted of nine couple. Mr Carter was then Secretary of the Club. Four couple came from the kennel of Mr Carter; 3 ½ couple from Mr George Krehl of Hanover Square, London; one couple from Mr C. Collett of 4 Selby-villas, Anerley, London; and half a couple from Mr F.D. Bland of Kippax Lodge, St. John's Wood-row, London. All were leading breeders and owners of the time and responsible for forming the Club.

The Kennel Review of March 1884 carried the following report on page 211:

> Mr Bland was assigned the duties of huntsman, and Messrs. Carter and Krehl were whips. Messrs. Krehl and Bland arrived with their hounds the night before, and in the morning early their hounds were sent into the large run attached to Mr Carter's kennels, in order that the two contingents might fraternise before entering on the duties. A start was made

> at twelve o'clock, and considering that the hounds from the various kennels had never before met as a pack, the smart trot of one mile to the Stour was accomplished with fairly good results, in regard to 'packing.'
>
> After crossing the Stour near the old Manor of Ravenscourt, now little more than a name, in the part of the old royal manor of Wye called Nacolt, the hounds were turned into a field well covered with reeds, and after drawing a blank proceeded in the direction of Wye for some thirty minutes, till on the summit of a hill near the winning-post of the old steeplechase course. Here the little hounds proclaimed, by the lusty way they gave tongue, that the hare was near, and, sure enough, in a few minutes the pack was in full cry. But, alas ! here a difficulty arose : the dogs could not be induced to respond to the huntsman's voice if their various owners were near, and so this first spin was in truth short, though, whilst it lasted, sweet. After more or less successful efforts to make the hounds pack better, we veered slightly round till close to the little village of Brook, with its quaint Norman tower, lately restored – and that not badly. Here we encountered some stiffish bits of plough and some broad brooks, which the hounds negotiated in fairly good style. No find here, so directing our course again to the right, we threw the pack into a field never yet known to fail when called upon for a hare.
>
> Sure enough, one hare and then another left its form: the pack, too excited, overran the scent, and again we met with a check. In picking up the scent again, part of the pack were seen disappearing after one hare and part meditating a chase after the other. The latter half were called off, but too late to enable us to get up with the rest, who eventually were lost to sight in a cover. Presently they appeared on the brow of a hill hard by, and it being thought better to learn the pack to keep together than to let one part go on alone, they were with some trouble called off.
>
> After re-uniting we proceeded into a large plough, and the hounds, at once giving tongue, told us we had another chance still before us, and so it was ; a capital run of forty-five minutes ensued, till the shades of evening told us we must turn towards home. Mr Bland made a capital huntsman, and had the latter part of last run to himself with seven hounds – Franco, Fino V., Ulfius, Brastias, Braconneau, Bellicent and Gipsy. Owing to the other hounds becoming stragglers, Mr Carter and Mr Krehl missed the best of this last run.
>
> But over the wine and walnuts we went over the day again, and were fain to come to the conclusion that the hounds were rare sportsmen, and though we had to be content with four views, three runs, but ne'er a kill, there was as not one but said it was an omen of better things, and that, given regular training and let the pack get accustomed to the voice of the huntsman only, the Basset-hound is a glorious dog, and ere long will vie with any hunt in England.

The success of this meet seems to have been repeated at least once as another meet took place in 1885 at Bishopstone, near Aylesbury under the Mastership of Mr Etherwood. But nothing more is known of other meets of the Club to its disbandment in 1925.

Mr Woodhouse's (1884–1890)

Mr A.N.L. Woodhouse lived in Liverpool. It is not known where he hunted. The first hound owned by him was Vulcan'84 by Lord Onslow's Fino (7850) out of Mr H. E. Munro's Nameless'83 (19485). Fino was bred in 1875 by the Comte le Couteulx in France and imported by Lord Onslow. About 1877 he was sold to Harry Ivon Jones, who later became Master of the Fairforth.

The Walhampton acquired two hounds from Mr Woodhouse as foundation stock: Absolute'90 (35500), and Adelaide'90 (35501). These were out of Woodhouse's

Busybody'86 and Woodhouse's Comus '87. There are indications that other of Mr Woodhouse's hounds were used by the Chiddingstone, the Delapré, the Danebury and the Highworth. Mr Woodhouse appears to have stopped breeding and showing bassets after 1890.

* *Danebury (1885–1890)*

Mornington Cannon (or Canon) was a race horse owner, who lived at Danebury, Hampshire. He is said to have imported hounds when he attended races in France. He and his son, Tom Mornington, were Masters of the pack. One of their first hounds was Jacometa (17118). It was probably purchased from Harry Ivon Jones, later Master of the Fairforth. Jacometa was from Lord Onslow's Cigarette (16541) by George Krehl's Bourbon (13853), both well known and prize winning hounds of the time.

About 1889, the Cannons imported six hounds from France: Boulougau, Mirant Rochambeau, Figaro, Ramette and Ravissante. The latter was a smooth coated basset bitch bred by Monsieur Louis Lane and it can be assumed that the others came from the same source. These hounds were slightly straighter in the leg and lighter than those of the Comte le Couteulx but from the same origins.

In 1890 or 1891, the Cannons sold their entire pack, 9½ or 10 couple, to Messrs. Christopher and Godfrey Heseltine, who were forming the Walhampton.

* *Riversdale (1886–1890)*

Mr Bulcock of Clitheroe, Lancashire, was the Master of the Riversdale bassets. One of his first hounds was Lycisca (21699), bred by Mr Ellis by Krehl's Fino VI (18100) out of Onslow's Citron (then owned by Mr Ellis). Several of his subsequent hounds had blood lines from George Krehl and Lord Onslow. Mr Bulcock had several successes in the show ring in the 1880s. There is no evidence of what became of his hounds after 1890.

* *Brighton (1887)*

Very little is known about this pack, except that it was owned by Major Croker of West Brighton in 1887. Two litters are given in the MBHA Stud Book. The first of two hounds were by a Mr Munro's Saucebox by Lord Onslow's Hermes. No pedigree is given for the second litter of two. Only one record of a Brighton hound can be traced. This is of 1892 and shows the Marchioness of Conygham of County Slane having a litter for the Walhampton from her Hettie by Brighton Benedict'87. This was at a time when the Walhampton had been sold to the Marquis of Conygham. It is possible that the Brighton was absorbed into the Brighton Beagles or were drafted to the Walhampton as Godfrey Heseltine knew the Major.

* *Dale Park (1888–1893)*

The Dale Park was formed in 1888 by Mr C. Fletcher. He obtained his stock mainly from well known breeders, including George Krehl, the Rev. P. Jackson and Mr G.B. Northcote. Little is known about the hunt. It seems to have been disbanded about 1893. Some of the hounds were drafted to the Wintershill and others may have gone to the Polebrooke.

* *Wintershill (1889–1896) Mr Moss's (1896–1898)*

The Wintershill was formed in 1889 by Mr J.S. Moss of Hampshire, with hounds drafted from the Danebury and later the Dale Park, as well as hounds from prominent breeders. In 1889 either alone or in conjunction with the Danebury, Mr Moss imported two bassets from Monsieur M. Hannoire: Rochambeau and Gibelotte. These were probably rough coated hounds.These two may have been drafted to the Danebury as Rochambeau sired four hounds for them in 1889. The pack seems to have changed its name to Mr Moss's in 1896 and entries in the MBHA Stud Book cease after this year. Mr Moss's appeared again in the *Field* as hunting in 1897–1898.

* *Walhampton (1890–1903; 1910–1914; 1920–1933)*

In 1890 the brothers Godfrey and Christopher Heseltine of Walhampton, Lymington in Hampshire were given one couple of basset hounds by Captain Peacock, who had been the Master of the Herefordshire and of the Isle of Wight Foxhounds. During the same year the brothers acquired three or four more couple. The MBHA Studbook lists four hounds for 1891. Two of these were later registered with the Kennel Club: Absolute'90 (35500) and Adelaide'90 (35511). They were both tricolour, smooth coated owned and bred by Mr A.N.L. Woodhouse in 1889. The other two may have been previously owned by Mr C. Lawrence and Everett Millais, both well known breeders of smooth coated bassets of the day. Later Godfrey Heseltine said: *'with four or five couples we used to chivey about.'*

They started the Hunt more formerly as The Walhampton in 1890 following their purchase of the entire stock, ten couple of smooth coated bassets, of the Danebury, owned by Mornington and Tom Cannon at nearby Stockbridge. The Cannons may have known the Heseltines through their mutual interest in horse breeding. Initially, the Heseltines hunted badger in the New Forest, by moonlight and in early morning.

The Heseltines switched to hare in September 1891 with Godfrey usually hunting them. During that year they acquired three couple of hounds from established breeders, including Mr Millais and ½ couple from the Riversdale. They considered the New Forest to be admirably suited to bassets as it was moorland and large open woodland but with some plough and banks around Lymington. Godfrey Heseltine later wrote: *'The heather on the moor is not sufficiently high to stop these little hounds and invariably carries good scent.'*

An idea of the hunting can be gained from Godfrey Heseltine's own accounts.

> In the New Forest, during the months of September, October, and early part of November, given a scent, the hounds can bring a hare to hand in 50 minutes to 1 hour 20 minutes. After the middle of November till the end of the season, I have scarcely ever hunted a hare to death in less than 2 hours, and it has much more often been 3 or 4 hours; it is very seldom that these hounds manage to kill a hare before she is so beat that you can pick her up yourself.
>
> They are very slow to take any advantage; sometimes they would rather throw their tongues than bite; in many cases beagles or even terriers would have killed a hare which has absolutely escaped from the jaws of the pack, because they are so slow to grasp the situation, or, more to the point, the hare."

Hounds were kept and fed in much the same way as Foxhounds of the time, except that they were given biscuit with their meal during the hunting season and were not fed meat, only the soup from horse flesh.

During the 1891–2 season and again during the 1892–3 season, the Walhampton hunted at Cambridge during term time, being kennelled at Chesterton and the remainder of the season in the New Forest and around Lymington. S. Walker was hired in 1891 as the Kennel Huntsman.

The Walhampton continued their policy of acquiring hounds from existing packs and leading breeders, culling out those that did not fit their needs. In 1895 they had Lurline (7931), by Walhampton Beauparc'92 out of Danebury Liberty. This hound Godfrey Heseltine considered to be influential in future breeding, although he was drafted before entry, to Mr Ruck (or Tom) Keene. Lurline produced two litters later used extensively by the Walhampton. They included: Fanchette'98; Felicia'98; Roderick'00 and Rosemary'00.

In the same year 1895 the Walhampton acquired Jollyboy'95 from Mr Everett Millais. Jollyboy was one of the results of the outcrossing carried out by Everett Millais between a basset and a Bloodhound. Millais's intention had been to improve the substance of the bassets and their heads.

The Walhampton also started to show in 1895, which allowed them to see more bassets and to contact breeders. It also gave them more opportunity to dispose of surplus hounds in their culling process. By 1896–1897 they had seventeen or more couple in kennels (about one-third dogs and two-thirds bitches) and were breeding five or six litters a year, but entering only ten or eleven couple per year. They were hunting about forty days a season and accounting for about seven-and-a-half brace of hares per season.

In 1896 Major Ferguson died and the entire ten couple of the Polebrooke were sold to the Walhampton by his executors. In the same year, Prince Henry of Pless gave the Walhampton ten couple from his pack in Germany. In 1899 the Walhampton acquired two hounds from another of the Millais outcrosses, Ada'94. These were Merryman'99 and Maisie'99. They were by Captain Evans' Music'96. Merryman'99 was used twice for breeding. One of the bitches put to Merryman'99 was Fanchette'98, by Lurline'95. Neither of the other half-crosses, Jollyboy'95 or Maisie'99 was used for breeding.Hunting was irregular during the 1899–1900 season as Godfrey was hunting

Walhampton, 1912.

the dog pack of the New Forest Foxhounds until January when he went to the South African Wars. Along with other Hunts the Walhampton did not hunt from 1900 to 1901.

Again in 1900, the Walhampton acquired two more Bloodhound crosses: Roderic'00 and Rosemary'00. They were by Captain Ruck Keene's Romulus'95 out of the favoured Lurline. Romulus'95 was another half-Bloodhound cross of Nicholas'93 x Innoculation. Rosemary'00 produced one litter. In 1907, for the Walhampton, Roderic'00 sired four litters for them in 1904 (2), 1905 and 1906. One of the 1904 litters was to the Lurline descendent, Felicia'98.

In the early 1900s the Walhampton continued its policy of acquiring hounds from packs and of acquiring hounds from leading show breeders, the Walhampton itself being active in the Show world. However, breeding was becoming more difficult. The basset was losing its popularity, partially because of the poor specimens being produced and partially because the number of packs began to decline generally throughout hunting. One reason for the poor breeding may have been the virtual cessation of importing dogs from Europe which followed the Quarantine Laws of 1901. This may have increased in-breeding. But the main reason was probably the rise in professional breeders producing dogs for sale rather than just for pleasure, which had inevitably led to much in-breeding. Matters were probably made worse by the growing public interest in Show results and the higher prices being asked for dogs. Godfrey Heseltine was particularly concerned about the decline in the constitution of bassets, putting the blame firmly on lack of knowledge, poor kennelling and ill thought out breeding policies. He had tried to improve matters in 1898 by introducing a points scale for judging. This differed from one already put forward by the BHC by placing more emphasis on build and limbs and less on coat, colouration and ears. In the early 1900s the Bloodhound outcross had caught the imagination of the show world and the Basset Hound was fast becoming a recognised breed.

In the 1890s the Walhampton first used some rough and smooth crosses bred by Mrs Tottie.This was repeated in 1902. The Walhampton had a litter sired by their smooth haired Ladas'99 out of a Mr F.M. Freake's half bred rough haired Holdford Venture. However, neither of these experiments produced satisfactory hunting hounds.

At the end of 1903 Godfrey Heseltine was called away for service with the Army in India. As a consequence, he sold the entire pack to his friend, the Marquis of Conygham, who created the Slane around them.

Godfrey Heseltine returned from India in 1909, moved to Billericay, Essex and became Master of the Essex Union Foxhounds. The Marquis of Conygham presented him with the Slane pack and the Walhampton was re-established at Billericay in 1910. His Kennel Huntsman was S. Hale. There were then sixteen couple of 13 to 14in smooth bassets in kennels. They usually met on Wednesday and Friday. The country was that of the Essex Union and had a lot of barbed wire.

During 1911 and 1912 the Walhampton introduced smooth coated basset blood from the Sandringham. By then most of their breeding was using their own stock because of the deterioration of most other sources and the rapid decline in popularity of the basset in the show ring.

At the outbreak of the Great War in1914 the pack was temporarily broken up. Five couple went to Lord Tredegar, five couple to Miss Daisy Ismay of the Iwerne, and five couple to Miss Gwynne Holford of the Buckland. Between 1916 and 1918 the pack was loaned to the Royal Navy at Rosyth, with Commander Hon. E. Nicholson RN as

Master. They were then sent to Reading with the Mastership between 1918 and 1920 being entrusted to Captain Cecil Aldin, the well known artist and writer, and Mr CH Carter of Purley, Berkshire. Throughout this period breeding continued using the limited stocks available to the hunts to which they had been dispersed.

In 1920 the pack was returned to Godfrey Heseltine. He had then re-located himself to Lutterworth, Leicestershire. There were ten couple of hounds. Godfrey hunted them and Kathleen Hinton was the Whipper-In. In 1921 he tried to help the BHC by entering hounds in a KC show. But their affairs had deteriorated so badly that they had to wind up the Club.

In 1921 Godfrey imported two Basset Artésien-Normand from France. This came about through correspondence with Monsieur Leon Verrier of Mont Saint-Aignan, near Rouen in co-authoring their book *'Les Bassets Français et leur Utilisation'* published in 1921. Monsieur Verrier believed that bassets were originally bred in the sixteenth century and were throwbacks to the St Hubert Hound by way of the French 'Chien d'ordre', large hunting hounds. He thought that bassets appeared in litters, were selected and inbred for their low character. These theories had heavily influenced breeding policies in England.

The hound imported from Monsieur Verrier was the bitch Pampente'21. Her sire was Farceur'19 from the Barly kennel of Monsieur Albert Mallart of Doullens, Somme, a long established breeder of Basset Artésien-Normand. The second hound imported was from Monsieur Verrier, the dog Meteor'21. The latter was used extensively by the Walhampton between 1923 and 1928, siring at least 7 litters. However, Pampente'21 seems to have been less well thought of only having a single litter in 1923 and only one dog from this litter being used, in 1927, and then only once.

From 1923 to 1929 the Walhampton bred almost exclusively from their own hounds, but for two entries in 1926 and another two in 1928 from the Dalby Hall and two in 1927 and one in 1929 from the Wick. During this time they were having five to eight litters a year and entering five to eight couples a year. In 1930 they excelled themselves with ten litters and twenty-six entries and used some Brancaster blood lines.

By 1932 they had thirty couple of hounds in kennels and were meeting twice a week. By then their hounds were highly prized and Walhampton Lymington'26 was sold in 1932 for £70. But tragedy struck when Godfrey died of gun shot wounds at his house. Mrs Heseltine took over the Mastership with Dr E.F.S. Morrison of Kibworth Beauchamp, Leicestershire. Dr Morrison had been whipping-in to the Walhampton for some seasons. Some of the Walhampton were auctioned at the Ladies Kennel Club show of 1932, Walhampton Abbot, Dipper and Lawless going to the US with Mr G Fearing. The remainder continued to hunt the 1932/3 season under Miss Mary Wills.

In 1933 Dr Morrison hunted the pack and Mrs Godfrey Heseltine showed some at Cruft's. But on the nineteenth May 1933 the remainder of the Walhampton were auctioned off at the Leicester Hound Sale, reaching very poor prices, averaging only £3 per hound. Dr Morrison purchased about twelve couple and these formed the nucleus of the Westerby. Amongst the other buyers were Mrs Edith Grew of Parkstone, Dorset with her Maybush kennels and Mrs Nina Elms of Andover, Hampshire with her Reynalton kennels. Both ladies went on to win many shows with their bassets. Other hounds were auctioned to breeders in France and the US.

** Polebrooke (1893–1896)*

Major V. Ferguson formed the Polebrooke, Northamptonshire in 1893, mainly from hounds of show breeders. About 1894, he imported a hound, Flambeau, from Monsieur

Bocquet of Paris. Monsieur Bocquet bred both crooked legged, rough haired Griffon bassets and Dachshunds and exhibited in England in the 1890s. In 1895 the Major used blood lines from the Dale Park and the Walhampton. The Major died in 1896 and the entire pack, fifteen couple, was sold to Messrs. Christopher and Godfrey Heseltine of the Walhampton. Some were retained by them, but about ten couple were sent to Mr B W Duff-Assheton-Smith in North Wales.

* *Cookridge (1893–1897)*

The pack was started about 1893 by a Mr J.A. Paul. Very little is known about the Hunt or Mr Paul. He may have been the James Andrew Paul who was married at the age of twenty in 1892 in Liverpool. The only village of a similar name is Cookbridge, near Lewes in Sussex.

The fifteen hounds recorded in the MBHA Stud Book from 1893 to 1897 were, with the exception of one litter of five bred from a Cookridge bitch, mainly bred by the Easthampstead. It is not known when and to where the hounds were dispersed after 1897.

* *Wheatley Park (1894–1899)*

Sir William Cooke of Wheatley Park, Doncaster, Yorkshire had bassets from at least 1892. In 1894 he formed the Wheatley Park. His hounds were mainly drafts from the Danebury and the Walhampton and some from leading breeders of the time. The pack ceased in 1899, possibly because of the South African Wars. Some of the hounds were probably drafted to the Delapré and the Eastington Park.

* *Delapré (1894–1904)*

Formed in 1894 by Messrs. C and R Cooper of Delapré Abbey, Northampton. They obtained their hounds from a variety of sources, mainly show breeders rather than hunts. H.A. Bryden in his book of 1903 writes that Pennel Elmshurst of the Brooksby said they looked like a first cross between a turnspit and a foxhound, but gave good music. *'The roar of nine couple would have drowned the combined dog-packs of the Pytchley, Grafton and Warwickshire'.* Bryden also says that bassets could be heard four miles down wind and that they could kill a hare in thirty-five minutes, breaking her up.

Elmshurst's comments may have been because, whilst the Delapré were predominantly smooth bassets, they had some outcross blood. Delapré Bella'96 was by Millais's Nicholas out of a Bloodhound, Swaffield's Guilder'94. Nicholas was one of the first bassets of Everett Millais and was said to be a highly inbred tricolour with a poor head. It was Nicholas that Millais used to artificially inseminate another Bloodhound in order to improve the structure of the basset. Delapré Phantom'97 was by Swaffield's Solomon'93 out of Mrs Tottie's Pervenche'92 (37741). Pervenche was a white and tan rough coated basset originally owned and imported by Monsieur Ernest Puissant of Merbes le Chateau, Belgium and bred in 1891 by Monsieur Bouquet.

The hunt seems to have been dispersed in about 1902–1904. There is some evidence that some of the hounds went to the Street Ashton.

Wolvercote (1895–1896)

Little is known about this Hunt other than that they hunted around Bishop's Waltham, Hampshire in the 1895–1896 season.

Mr B.W. Duff-Assheton-Smith's (1896)

Mr Smith resided at Vaynol Park, Bangor, Gwneydd. He received ten couple of hounds from the Polebrooke when they ceased in 1896. It is believed that they were drafted to Sir Bromley-Wilson of the Dallam Tower and to the Marquis of Conygham of the Slane.

** Highworth (1896–1900)*

Mr C.E. Hanbury of Highworth in Wiltshire owned a basset hound, Lord George (37723) in 1894. The pack may have been formed in 1896 or 1897. The foundation stock seems to have come from breeders, including a blood line from Everett Millais. Subsequently stock was probably obtained from the Walhampton. The pack seems to have been disbanded by 1900. It is not known where the hounds went.

** Chiddingstone (1897–1903)*

Formed in 1897 by Mr E.H.M. Denny of Chiddingstone Castle, Eden Bridge, Kent, possibly for his daughters. Their first hound was Royalty (23H) a tan and white hound bred in 1896 by Captain Owen Swaffield by an imported hound, Statesman (unregistered), out of a tricolour bitch Saracenesca (41782), both owned and bred by Captain Swaffield. Their next hound was Lockinge (28H), a tan and white hound bred by Arthur Croxton-Smith in 1899 by his Wantage (99D) out of Captain Swaffield's Spinster.

The pack was built up over the years by drafts from the Walhampton and the Delapré, as well as further hounds from Captain Swaffield and Arthur Croxton-Smith. By 1902 there were fourteen couple kennelled at Chiddingstone Castle run by the kennel huntsman, Mr Frederick Theobald, hunting on Mondays and Thursdays. They were hunted by Mr Denny and Mr T. Duke. The hunt seems to have ceased after 1903. Some of the hounds seem to have been drafted to the Slane.

In the late 1960s, the author met an elderly man who recalled how he and his father had worked with the hounds. One of their duties was to carry home bassets at the end of the day on hurdles as they were so exhausted!

Moyola Park(1898–1899)

This pack was owned by Lieutenant-Colonel R. Spencer of Templepatrick, co. Down, Ireland. The hounds were probably kennelled at his house under the Kennel Huntsman, Frank Favis. The Hunt was formed sometime before 1900, at which time it was changed to beagles because the bassets were unable to get over the stone walls and deep bog drains and were not fast enough. Where the bassets came from and where they went are not known. They may have been from the Slane. The country hunted lay in counties Antrim and Derry. It mainly consisted of pasture, moorland and bog with a little plough and woodland, without much barbed wire.

*Sir Maurice Bromley-Wilson's (1898–1913) * Dallam Tower (1914)*

The pack was formed in 1898 by Sir Maurice Bromley-Wilson of Dallam Tower, Milnthorpe, Westmoreland. He may also have had drafts from the Walhampton. It was originally known as Sir Maurice Bromley-Wilson's Bassets and re-named at the outbreak of WW1 in 1914. Sir Maurice was a Founder Member of the MBHA in 1911. As well as hunting, Sir Maurice was a leading participant with bassets in the show ring and seems to have bred and owned some bassets before forming the pack. His original bassets came from show breeders. But, in 1904, he started to use Walhampton bloodlines, together with lines developed by Arthur Croxton-Smith. In 1912 and 1913 he used Sandringham Zero'10 as a stallion. Zero was a smooth basset owned and bred by Queen Alexandra in 1909 and a frequent prize winner. Almost all his hounds were tricolour. The pack consisted of fifteen couple of smooth bassets, kennelled at Dallam Tower. They were hunted by Sir William. The Hon. Secretary to the hunt was R.M. Deighton of Elmsfield, Milnthorpe. Sir William's Kennel Huntsman was William Jackson. It is not known how the pack was dispersed at the outbreak of WWI. Some may have gone to the Wroxton.

** Knowlton (c. 1900)*

Miss Gladys Peto lived at Knowlton, near Canterbury, Kent. In 1900 she formed the Knowlton. The whippers-in were her two sisters and a brother. Nothing else is known about this pack and the records were destroyed by fire in 1923. One of her hounds, a tan and white, Gaily (KC Reg. 26H) went to the Walhampton, but was not used for breeding, as far as is known.

Colonel Reynardson's (c. 1900) .

All that is known is that they hunted around Stamford, Rutland soon after 1900.

Mr Vincent Eyre's (c. 1900)

All that is known is that they hunted around Nuneaton, Warwickshire soon after 1900.

** Stoodleigh (1900–1901)*

All that is known is that they were hunting in Devon in the 1900–1901 season under their Master, Mr E.H. Dunning.

** Street Ashton (1902)*

The MBHA Stud Book records four entered hounds for 1902 under the Mastership of Mr Q.O. Gold. The hounds seem to have been drafts from the Delapré and may have been disposed of to the Slane and the Stainrigg.

** Reepham (1902–1903)*

The Reepham appear to have existed for one season, 1902–1903. The Masters were Messrs. N.C. and H.C. Swan, with Mr N.C. Swan hunting them. They were kennelled at Reepham, Lincolnshire with the Kennel Huntsman, Charles Freeman. They had ten couple of basset hounds and hunted twice a week. They may have had obtained hounds from the Walhampton. It is not known where the hounds went.

** Stainrigg (1902–1912) Argyll & Sutherland Highlanders (1912-?)*

Started in 1902 by Mr J. Little of Stainrigg, Berwickshire, Scotland. Hounds were owned by Mr Little and kennelled at his house. He had ten couple of 12 to 14in smooth basset hounds, some of which were entered in the KC Stud Book. Some were drafts from the Street Ashton. Others may have come from breeders of the time, including Mr Arthur Croxton-Smith. They were also drafted from the Dallam Tower, Riversfield, Greywell Hill and Wroxton. They met on various days. The country lay in the countries of the Duke of Buccleuch's and the Berwickshire and was almost entirely plough.

In 1912 they became the Regimental Pack of the Argyll and Sutherland Highlanders at Fort George. Nothing is known about what happened to this pack.

*Winchfield (1902–1910) * Greywell Hill (1911–1914)*

The pack was formed in 1902 as the Winchfield in Hampshire, probably by Captain the Honourable Dudley Carleton, later Lord Dorchester. He was one of the original members of the MBHA. Between 1904 and 1906, the Master was the Marquis of Devonshire. By 1911 the hounds were kennelled at Greywell Hill, near Basingstoke, Hampshire under the Kennel Huntsman, F. Loffe, and the name changed. The country hunted was in that of the Garth, H.H. and Vine Foxhounds. They met two days a week on Tuesday and Saturday. It was a private pack owned by the Master with no subscriptions. The hounds were fifteen couple of 14in smooth coated bassets. Initially stock came from breeders, including Arthur Croxton-Smith. Later blood lines of established packs were used, including the Dallam Tower, the Walhampton and Slane. The hunt was disbanded in 1914 with some hounds being drafted to Mr Fleming's. By 1925 Lord Dorchester had lost all records.

Their most famous hound was Dalby Hall Dorchester '09, winner of the MBHA 1914 Show, when it belonged to Mr Fleming. Dorchester was described as: *one of the handsomest Bassets of modern times.* Between 1911 and 1916, he sired 53 registered hounds in 16 litters.

Major Kemmis's (c. 1903)

All that is known is that that Major Kemmis resided in Portarlington, Co. Leix, Ireland.

Mr Baylay's (c. 1903)

All that is known is that that Mr Baylay resided in Monte, Co. Westmeath, Ireland.

** Slane (1903–1910)*

The Slane Castle Bassets were started in the early 1890s by the Marchioness of Conygham, Slane Castle, co. Meath. In 1892 the Walhampton had a litter out of the Marchioness's Hettie. It is possible that the Marquis obtained his first bassets as drafts from Mr Duff-Assheton-Smith. It appears that they were loaned to the Royal Naval College at Osborne for a time.

When he left for India in 1903, Captain Godfrey Heseltine sold the Walhampton to the Marquis of Conygham, the son of the Marchioness as he considered the Marquis *'to be infallible'*. The Hunt was known as the Slane with the Marquis as sole Master and were shown as well as hunted. In 1910 Godfrey Heseltine returned from India and the Marquis presented the hounds to him to resume the Walhampton.

** Riversfield (1903–1913)*

The Hunt was established as a private pack in 1903 owned Mr A.F. Towgood, of Riversfield, St. Neots, Huntingdon. They hunted over the Cambridgeshire and Oakley Foxhounds country. The country was predominantly plough with some pasture and a little woodland. They met on Monday and Friday. The hounds were kennelled at his house. Initially, Messrs. Towgood and Peppercorn acted as Kennel Huntsmen. In 1909 S. Stamford was appointed as Kennel Huntsman. They had ten couple of 14in rough and smooth haired basset hounds. The predominant blood line was Walhampton, with some Greywell Hill blood. The Huntsman was a Mr H.S. Towgood. They claim to have accounted for sixteen hares per season initially. This tally rose to thirty-five per season by 1909. The Hunt was disbanded in 1913.

* *Dalby Hall (1906–1931)*

The Dalby Hall were started in 1906 by Captain, later Colonel, Burns-Hartopp of Dalby Hall, Melton Mowbray, Leicestershire, following his relinquishment of the Mastership of the Quorn Foxhounds. He was a Founder Member of the MBHA. He died in 1954. His daughter, Miss Lettice Burns-Hartopp, was Master and huntsman. She later edited the MBHA Stud Book from 1932 to 1938. The pack was formed from hounds presented to them by the Greywell Hill and the Slane. They continued to use bloodlines from these two packs and the Walhampton until 1925.

During the 1916–19 season the hounds were loaned to the Grand Fleet at Rosyth and kennelled near Dunfermline. In 1926 they were on loan to Captain R.F.P. Monckton of Stretton Hall, Stafford. Captain Monckton had started a pack of Beagles in that year and hunted the Albrighton country. In 1927 they were on loan to a Major Hodgkin and in 1928 they were loaned to the Wick and District. The pack was disbanded in 1931. Some of the hounds appear to have gone to the Walhampton, Eastington Park and Waltham.

The pack originally consisted of 15 ½ couple of 12–14in smooth bassets. These were later reduced to 11 ½ couple. The kennel huntsman was Alfred Felstead, who was succeeded in 1921 by C. Aberfield. Whippers-in originally were Miss D. Burns-Hartopp and Alfred Felstead, then Tom Cooper and then W. Longden. Hounds met three days a fortnight.

In 1923 the Dalby Hall imported Vannette'23 from France, bred by Monsieur M. Hannoire by his Domino de Morguy out of his Syntaxe de Morguy. This bitch whelped one litter in 1925. In 1889 the Danebury had imported four hounds and the Wintershill had imported two from Monsieur Hannoire. It is thought that Monsieur Hannoire may have bred rough haired bassets. Bloodlines from these were used by basset packs in the USA, notably the Staridge, Maple Drive and Nottke. Mrs Elizabeth Streeter, who formed the Skycastle, maintained that some of the long hair encountered in US bassets came from this bloodline.

Sitka (1902–1908)

Also referred to as the 'Litka' and the 'Zitka'. Probably owned, hunted and kennelled by Major D. Teichman, DSO, MC of 'Sitka', Eltham, Kent. They hunted over the West Kent country around Chislehurst. At some time the Mastership may have moved to a Mr MacIntyre. At the cessation of the Sitka the Fairforth were formed and took over their country. Hounds may have been drafted to the Fairforth.

* *North Lancashire (1907–1910) Captain Olive's (1910–1911)*

The Hunt was formed in 1907 as a private pack and owned by the Masters, Captain Y.B. Olive of 'The Buffs' and Mr T.B. Forwood, by purchase of hounds from Mr J.L. Wordsworth of the 5th Lancers. Captain Olive seems to have bred bassets in 1905 and two of his breeding were owned by a Mrs O.M. Olive, possibly his wife, who lived at Sunnyside, Leicester. In 1910, Mr E.S Beadon became Kennel Huntsman. Initially, they had about twelve couple of 12 to 14in rough and smooth Basset hounds. The uniform for Hunt Servants was a green coat with a white collar. By 1909 the pack had increased to fifteen couple and the Hunt was meeting twice a week. In 1910 the name of the pack was changed to Captain Olive's. Captain H.K. Clough of Sunnyhill, Lancaster had been appointed Hon. Secretary. He also whipped in. The number of hounds had been reduced to six couple. They had introduced an evening dress of knee beeches and silk stockings with buckled shoes, together with a green dress coat with

Capt. Y.B. Olive's Artful, 1911. Formerly the North Lancashire Bassets.

green linings and white facings. The pack was kennelled in Lancaster, possibly in the barracks. The uniform for Hunt Servants was green with a white collar. They hunted north of Lancashire, south of the Vale of Lune Harriers, on Wednesday and Saturday. Their country was almost entirely pasture. The Kennel Huntsman was Tim Houlihan and the whipper-in was Mr L.B. Forwood. They had a hunt button and allowed subscribers (1 guinea) to wear it. The hunt appears to have been disbanded about 1911. Several of the hounds appear to have been drafted to the Fairforth.

* *Wroxton (1907–1933)*

Lord North of Wroxton Abbey, Banbury, Oxfordshire turned to bassets following a fall which left him unable to ride. As a result he formed his own private pack, the Wroxton, in 1907. He followed his bassets in a waggonette driven by an old hunt servant, getting out and proceeding on foot when the driving got too difficult. The foundation stock were drafts from the Walhampton, the Greywell Hill and the Dallam Tower. The latter two supplied the bulk of all future lines. The hounds were described as being *'shorter in the leg and more snipey than the Walhampton'*. The Hon. Secretary was Colonel the

Lord North and the Wroxton, 1920, on his 84th birthday.

Hon. W.F. North of Wroxton House, Banbury. The hounds were kennelled at Wroxton Park under the Kennel Huntsman Stephen Giles. There were fifteen couple of 13in bassets belonging to the Master. They were said to be small and active with good bone. They generally hunted on Tuesday and Saturday, by invitation of the Master. The country was mainly in Warwickshire but some hunts were in the Bicester & Heythrop countries. It was pasture and plough and had no barbed wire. The Hunt kept going during the 1914–1918 War and provided recreation for soldiers on leave from the Front.

In 1927 a hunt uniform was adopted as a brown velveteen coat with a plush waistcoat and black vulcanite buttons with 'W.B.H' engraved in silver. In 1928 the Kennel Huntsman, Stephen Giles, was replaced by Fred Giles, who had been whipping-in. The hounds did not hunt during the 1930–1931 season when Lord North fell ill. The pack was disbanded in 1933, most hounds going to Scotland.

Lord North was born in 1836 and died in 1933 at the age of ninety-seven. He had been an outstanding figure in the hunting world. He was Joint Master of the Warwickshire Foxhounds from 1861 to 1866 and Master of the Bicester Foxhounds from 1866 to 1870. He was one of the Founder Members of the MBHA in 1911 and was elected as the first President. His niece, Miss Winifred Fitzgerald, became Secretary of the MBHA.

Lord North, Master of the Wroxton, 1925, agen 89.

Mursley (1908–1910)

Formed in 1908 as a subscription pack by the Master and Huntsman, Viscount Malden of Leighton Buzzard, Buckinghamshire. Mr S.S. Green of Leighton Buzzard was Hon. Secretary. Hounds were kennelled at the Master's house. It is not known where the hounds were obtained from or what became of them. They met on Monday and Friday. The minimum subscription was one guinea or a cap of 2s.6d. The country was in the territory of the Whaddon Chase Foxhounds and was also hunted over by Lord Rothschild's Stag hounds. It was nearly all grass and with little wire. In 1910 the pack was re-formed with Beagles as Lord Malden's.

* *Buckland (1908–1912)*

Very little is known about this pack, except that it was owned by Miss Nell Gwynne Holford in 1908 with hounds that appear to have been bred by the Walhampton or Slane. In the MBHA Stud Book there is mention of the Walhampton using hounds belonging to a Mr Freake with the prefix Holford. In 1914 Godfrey Heseltine sent five couple of the Walhampton to the Buckland as part of his strategy to disperse his hunt during the Great War. The hounds were collected together in 1918 and initially sent to Reading until they returned to Godfrey Heseltine in 1920.

Whether or not there is a connection, *Baily's Directory* has an entry for the Buckland Beagles saying that they would not be hunting the 1915–16 Season. According to notes of Mr Scott-Willey, Master of the Worcester Park Beagles, the Master of the Buckland Beagles returned to his Regiment in 1914 at the outbreak of War. During the 1914–15 season the hounds were hunted by the Kennel Huntsman, Flander, with Mr J.E. Humprey acting as Field Master. In 1915 the Committee decided to put down the old hounds and trencher-feed the remainder. The latter seems not to have succeeded. The Minute Book showed that all hounds were disposed of, hence the entry in *Baily's*. The Buckland Beagles hunted from Reigate. After a series of mergers they and the Worcester Park became part of the present day Surrey and North Sussex Beagles.

* *Fairforth (1909–1916)*

The Hunt was established in 1909 by Mr F. H. Temperley on the cessation of the Sitka Basset hounds, possibly by drafts from this Hunt. It is not known whether or not this Mr Temperley was related to the brothers John and Reginald Temperley. They were involved with bassets and Dachshunds in the 1870s and 1880s and known to Everett Millais.

In 1910 the hounds were purchased by Mr Harry Ivon (or Ivan) Jones of Eltham, Kent for a private subscription pack. Mr Jones also showed hounds. The Secretary was Mr Glenton Roslin Williams of Sidcup, Kent, who had hunted them under Mr Temperley. Their country adjoined that of the West Kent Foxhounds. The Hunt took over a large portion of the West Kent Harriers country, running parallel with the river as far as Cobham, also a small portion at Keston and Down in the Old Surrey country. This country mainly consisted of plough land with some pasture and a little woodland. It included hop fields. In 1913 Mr Jones was joined, as Joint Master, by Mr A.E Leonard, of Sidcup. The hunt met on Saturdays, with occasional Wednesdays. The subscription was two guineas to wear a large Hunt button and one guinea to wear a small Hunt button. The kennels were originally at Sidcup Station. In 1926 the kennels moved to Burnt Oak Lane, Lamorbey, Sidcup with the West Kent Harriers, which had become the Badlesmere Foot Harriers by 1911. The first Kennel Huntsman was L.

The Fairforth in the Kent Hop Fields, 1910.

Mercer. In 1912 he was succeeded by David Shepherd. The Fairforth used Riversfield blood lines extensively in the early 1900s. About 1910 they imported Gaylass from France. They had eleven couple of rough & smooth bassets. Between 1916 and1917, the hounds were distributed among other packs whilst David Shepherd was away on active service. This probably included Gaylass (the imported hound) which went the Dalby Hall. The Hunt does not seem to have survived the War.

** Mr V Fleming's (1911–1915)*

Major Valentine Fleming of Brazier's Park, Ipsden, Oxfordshire was an MP and formed a pack in 1911 by purchase of the Greywell Hill. He was one of the original members of the MBHA. Unfortunately, the Major was killed in the Great War and the pack was disbanded in 1915 and sold to Major Hessy of Drury Lodge, Colchester. The Major's Stud Book was lost during the Great War.

Iwerne Minster (1913–1917)

In 1913 Miss Daisy Ismay of Iwerne Minster House, Blandford, Dorset formed a private pack kennelled at her residence under the Kennel Huntsman, T. Church, with herself as Master and Huntsman. In that year she showed at the MBHA show at Banbury. At the outbreak of War Godfrey Heseltine sent five couple of hounds from the Walhampton to her. By 1915 there were ten-and-a-half couple in kennels. They were 16in dog hounds and 14in bitch hounds. They hunted on Wednesday and Saturday. The country was in that of Lord Portman's Foxhounds and consisted mainly of pasture with some plough, but no wire. The Hunt seems to have ceased in 1917. The hounds may have been returned to the Walhampton.

** Lord Tredegar's (1914–1933)*

Lord, later Viscount, Tredegar of Tredegar Park, Newport, Gwent started the Hunt in 1914 with a pack of 'close coated' bassets. He had been one of the founder members of the MBHA in 1911. The Hon. Secretary of the Hunt was Major B.D. Corbet. The majority of his hounds were of Walhampton descent. Ten couple of hounds were kept at Tredegar Park in the charge of the Kennel Huntsman, Walter Barrett. They hunted on Tuesday and Friday.

At the outbreak of the Great War, the Walhampton was temporarily broken up. Some of their hounds went to Lord Tredegar. After the War, in 1919, Lord Tredegar gave the Royal Tank Corps some of his hounds to start their Hunt. In 1928 the pack was resuscitated by purchase of a draft from the Walhampton. In 1933 the entire pack was sold at the Leicester Repository Hound Sale, along with the remainder of the Walhampton. Some were purchased by Col. E.F.S. Morrison when he started the Westerby.

Tank Corps (1919–1922)
** 3rd Battalion, Royal Tank Corps (1923–1926)*

The Hunt was formed on 20 May 1919 at Bovington Camp, Wool, Dorset with a draft of hounds from Lord Tredegar and was originally known as the Tank Corps Basset Hounds. The first Master and Huntsman was Captain L.B. Ball. In 1920, he was succeeded by Major G. McClintock, DSO. In 1923 the Hunt moved to Lydd Camp, Kent and became known as the 3rd Battalion, Royal Tank Corps Basset Hounds. The Mastership was changed to Lieutenant Colonel F.R. Hope, CBE, DSO. In 1925 he was succeeded by Lieutenant D.F.M. Tudor. The Kennel Huntsman at Bovington was Private Downes. He was succeeded in 1920 by Private Walker. On the move to Lydd, Private J. Absalom became Kennel Huntsman and Whipper-In. Initially they had fourteen couple of hounds. This was reduced to seven-and-a-half when they moved to Lydd. The pack was maintained by subscriptions from the officers of the Corps., as well as private donations. There was a cap of 2s.6d levied on all, other than members of the Tank Corps. At Bovington they met on Monday, Wednesday and Friday. This was reduced to Tuesday and Friday at Lydd. At Bovington they hunted in Dorset in a country next to that of the South Dorset Foxhounds. The Hunt appears to have been disbanded in about 1926. Some hounds may have gone to the Brancaster.

*Miss Ena Adam's (1923–1926) * Brancaster (1927–1933)*

Miss Edna Adams of Cowesby Hall, Northallerton, Yorkshire originally had a pack of beagles. She was the daughter of Norman Adams, a well known hound judge and a Master of Foxhounds. In 1923 the beagles were changed to bassets and known as Miss Ena Adam's Bassets. Miss Adams was Master and Huntsman. Her brother, Mr N.J. Adams was the whipper-in. The hounds were kennelled at Cowesby Hall and were originally five couple of black and white Basset Hounds presented to her by Mr R.W.R. Mackenzie of Earlshall, Fife. They hunted on Thursday and bye-days. No subscription or cap was taken. The country was chiefly in the Bilsdale area with pasture, plough and a lot of moorland, but no wire. Miss Adams hunted them on horseback. In 1926 the kennels were moved to Stratton, near Cirencester, Gloucestershire under the Kennelman, Frank Burns. Hunting was on Monday and bye-days. The country was that of the Royal Agricultural College Beagles of pasture and plough. The number of hounds had been increased to eight couple.

In 1927 the hunt was moved to Brancaster Hall, King's Lynn, Norfolk and was renamed the Brancaster and Messrs. H. Simms and N. Adams became Joint Masters. The Hon. Secretary was Mr Norman J. Adams. The Kennel Huntsman was A. Capell. They were then hunting two or three days a week. The new country was mainly light plough, around Hunstanton. Miss Adams continued to hunt them on horseback. Her father toured France looking for new stock, but was appalled at the poor standard of bassets in France at that time. As a result of this it is thought that she obtained some hounds from Count de Berthe in France. Miss Adams used these to change her breeding policy to hounds of an 18in height, but retaining the black and white marking. She continued to draw upon Mr and Mrs MacKenzie's blood lines, as well as using some from the Dalby Hall, the Walhampton and Mrs Nina Elms. Miss Adams said of her hounds:

> As I hunt a plough country, I hunt on horseback, and have gradually bred my hounds up to eighteen inches high on straight legs, but in all other characteristics they are pure bassets and have simply been evolved by selective breeding. I think it shows that years back the basset as imported from France by Sir Edward Millais in 1874 was in fact bred down in the course of centuries by the French from their grand Chien de Chasse, and can therefore with care be bred back again to that type if desired.

The pack was disbanded in 1932 or 1933. She initially gave her hounds to Lord Cadogan, who later returned them to the Westerby.

* *Wrest Park (1924–1925)*

The Wrest Park were formed in 1924 by the Master and Huntsman, Mr John G. Murray of Wrest Park, Ampthill, Bedfordshire. The Hunt uniform was a green coat with a blue collar and brass buttons inscribed 'W.B.H.', green stockings and a black velvet cap. Hounds were kennelled at Wrest Park under A.J. Ling, the Kennel Huntsman. They consisted of ten couple of hounds belonging to the Master , drafted from the Dalby Hall and Walhampton. Hunting was irregular and they only hunted the one season.

* *Wick and District (1924–1936)*

The Wick and District Beagles were formed in 1909 by the Master, Dr J.H. Hawes, of Wick near Bristol, Gloucestershire. They were disbanded in 1914 due to the War. In 1924 Dr Hawes revived them as a subscription basset pack with Mr E.E. Pratt of Pucklechurch, near Bristol, as Joint Master. The former was Huntsman and the latter was Hon. Secretary. The hounds were kennelled at Wick in charge of R. Knapp as Kennel Huntsman. They had nine-and-a-half couple belonging to the Committee. The hounds appear to have been drafts from the Dalby Hall.

In 1928 Major C. Wade became Joint Master with Mr Pratt. Mark Whitwell of Pucklechurch became Hon. Secretary. Major Wade took on the hunting. Both had been whipping-in from the formation. In 1931 the Joint Mastership changed again , taken by Mr J. Seymour Williams of Warmley and Mr L. Phipps, with Mr Seymour Williams hunting hounds, having been whipping-in since 1928. In 1932 the Kennel Huntsman changed to H.A. Frost and the kennels had moved to Warmley. They met on Wednesday and Saturday. The country hunted was mainly pasture with some plough, mainly around Bath, Bristol and Chipping Sodbury. The minimum subscription was two guineas and a cap was taken.

By 1933 the pack had grown to twenty couple. In 1936 the bassets were disposed of and the Cranwell Beagles purchased. The name was changed to the Wick Beagles. Many of the bassets were drafted to the Westerby. One, Wick Welcome'35, was acquired by Miss M.M. Keevil who used him to build up her pack and form the Grims.

* *Major Wilkie's (1928–1929)*

The pack was formed in 1928 with a draft from the Dalby Hall. It appears to have disbanded the following year.

** Eastington Park (1928–1940)*

This private pack was formed in 1928 by the Master and Huntsman, Major Claude de Lisle Bush of Eastington Park, Stonehouse, Gloucestershire. The hounds were drafted from the Walhampton and kennelled at Eastington Park under the Kennel Huntsman J.Scarratt. There were fourteen couple of hounds belonging to the Master. They hunted on Monday and Friday. The uniform was a brown velvet coat with gilt buttons engraved 'E.P.B.H.' and a yellow waistcoat. The pack was gradually built up, with predominant use of Walhampton blood and occasional Brancaster and Wick. By 1936 there were twenty couple and this rose to twenty-four couple in 1938. But, following the outbreak of War in 1939 the pack was disbanded in 1940. Some of the hounds went to the Scalford Hall and to the Willoughby to keep hunting going through the War years.

** Waltham (1933–1937)*

These were formed in 1933 by the Hon. Mrs Edward Greenall. In 1934, she imported Comedy'34 from France. There this hound was known as Mistinguette in France and had been bred by Monsieur Auguste Mallart of Doullens, Somme from his famous Barly kennels of Basset Artésien-Normand. In 1935 the pack had a draft from the Walhampton but it was disbanded in 1937.

** Westerby (1933–1939; 1944 to present)*
Willoughby (1939–1944)

In 1932 Dr Eric F.S. Morrison of St Glen, Leicestershire, became Master of the Walhampton, having whipped into them for some years. Following the tragic death of their founder, Godfrey Heseltine, Eric hunted them for one season and then purchased much of the remaining pack when they were sold at Leicester Repository in 1933. He then changed the name to Westerby as the name Walhampton was the registered prefix to the gundogs of Christopher Heseltine. The twelve couple of hounds belonging to the Master were kennelled at St. Glen under the Kennel Huntsman, R Wilford. The Hon. Secretary was Mrs W.G. Coates of Rugby. The country covered those of the Fernie, Pytchley and Atherstone Foxhounds (of which Eric was a Master) and had very little plough. Meets were on Saturday, with bye-days. A full subscription was three guineas, an ordinary subscription two guineas and a family subscription was five guineas. There was a cap of 2s.6d. The hunt uniform was a brown coat with a Padua red collar. The pack was gradually built up with some Brancaster and Wick blood lines introduced. By 1938 there were twenty couple of hounds. A new Kennel Huntsman had been appointed, R. Hill. In 1937 Lieutenant Colonel G.A.C. Breitmeyer was appointed as Joint Master. In 1938 Miss J. Oram of Knighton Hall, Leicestershire took over as Hon. Secretary.

The outbreak of War saw Eric Morrison take up his military duties. The pack was loaned to the seventeenth Lancers at the Training Centre, Tidworth, under the Mastership of Major Fitzhugh, who became Master of the Belvoir. They were later loaned to Northamptonshire Yeomanry under the Mastership of Mr Lowinger until 1944. Some were drafted to Colonel F.G.D. Colman, OBE, TD. to form the Scalford Hall. Miss Keevil told the author that Colonel Morrison arrived one day at the outbreak of WWII with a horse-box. He left her with some hounds and two of his horses with the strict instructions that, if feed got difficult, the horses were to be fed to the hounds!

During the War until 1944, the reduced pack was hunted as the Willoughby. Eric Morrison was one of the original members of the Desert Rats (7th Armoured Division) serving as a Doctor. He was awarded the Military Cross at the second battle of Tobruk and four times mentioned in despatches. Between 1939 and 1947 the affairs of the Hunt were kept going by a Committee.

It was not until 1947 that the Hunt could fully operate again with hounds returned from their various dispersal places, especially the Willoughby. Mr Kingsley Gimson of Stoneygate House, Leicestershire and Mr R.P. Swain of Bunker's Hill, Burton Overy joined Eric Morrison as Joint Masters and Mrs Swain took on the duties of the Hon. Secretary. Fourteen couple of hounds were now kennelled at Pappilon Hall, Lubenham, Market Harborough, Leicestershire. Meets were held on Tuesday and Saturday. Subscriptions were kept at five guineas, but the cap was raised to five shillings. Eric Morrison returned to hunting them and A. Whittaker was appointed as Kennel Huntsman. He was soon replaced by E.C. Taylor.

Breeding hounds was difficult as only the Scalford Hall and the Castle Milk survived the War. The Scalford Hall soon disbanded and the Castle Milk had some rough coated lines. One consequence was that lines from breeders of show Basset Hounds had to be used, particularly Miss Keevil's Grims, Miss Nina Elm's Reynalton and Mrs Walley's. At that time the basset world in England was very small and everybody had the one interest in building hounds up again. More significantly, between 1949 and 1952, Eric Morrison made various outcrosses with a view to improving the constitution of the basset for hunting, without diminishing either the scenting ability or cry. His first experiment was using a beagle stud dog: Trinity Foot Marksman'46. This proved unsuccessful. He then tried outcrosses with harrier, notably Dunston Gangway'48. This proved to be much more helpful to achieving his aims. Many of the first cross were subsequently used for breeding, notably Redskin'50, Galliard'50, Clinker'51 and Gaelic'52. By 1950, the Westerby had built up sufficient stock to be able to rely mainly on home breeding. It was these outcrosses that established the 'Westerby' type of hound that dominated the basset hunts in the UK for many years and became known as the English Basset. In 1959 Eric Morrison writing to George Johnston and said: '*I am responsible chiefly for the dreadful crime of crossing the Basset with other hound breeds. I would like you to know that I did this solely to keep the breed alive, as in the middle thirties it was in danger of becoming extinct.*'

Unfortunately Eric Morrison died in 1951. Mr C.A. Weston of Great Bowden, Market Harborough, Leicestershire took on the Mastership and became the Huntsman. He continued the breeding policy of Eric Morrison. Mrs Josephine Groom of Foxton, Market Harborough became Hon. Secretary. J. Coulthard was appointed as Kennel Huntsman. In 1953 Mrs Weston took over as Hon. Secretary and was succeeded in 1955 by Colonel A.G. Stewart of Rugby. In that year the kennels were moved to Mr Weston's. In 1955 S. Philips became Kennel Huntsman.

In 1956 Mr J.C.E. Bevin of Welford, Rugby became Joint Master with Mr Weston. In 1959 Mr Bevin became sole Master when Mr Weston retired. In that year a beagle outcross was once again tried. This time the dog hound North Warwickshire Redwing'56 was used. Whilst this seems to have been not a great success as the progeny were never used for breeding, the outcross was tried again in 1960 with the beagle stud dog North Warwickshire Goliath'57. This seems to have been more suitable as several of the progeny were subsequently used for breeding, especially Godfrey'60. One of the progeny, Remedy'62, was drafted to the Tewksbury in the USA and had at least one litter.

In 1960 the kennels were moved to Saddington, Leicestershire, the home of Mr J.J.L. Underwood, who joined Mr Bevin as Joint Master for one season in 1963. In 1962 J. Stewart-Peter of Knossington, Oakham, Rutland had become Joint Hon. Secretary. By then the subscription was ten guineas for a family and seven guineas for an individual, the cap remained at five shillings. In 1965 the beagle outcross was tried again, this time with the dog hound Per Ardua Bluecap. This seems to have been successful in that one of the progeny, Billesdon'65, was used as a stud dog in 1970. In 1966 the hounds were put in a Trust and became the property of the country. In 1967 the kennels were moved again, this time to Walcote Road, South Kilworth, near Market Harborough. In 1973 J. Atkinson was appointed as Kennel Huntsman.

In 1976 Dr Duncan Jeffry of Thurleston, near Rugby was appointed as Chairman and Miss D.M. Hirst of Newton Harcourt, Leicestershire became Hon. Secretary. In the following year Mrs Carol Thursfield of Wilbarston, near Market Harborough, Leicestershire became Joint Hon. Secretary. In 1978 Mr David B. Bragg of Clifton, Dunsmore, Rugby became Joint Master and hunted hounds in the following year.

In the 1983/4 season, the mid week meet was on Wednesday, instead of Tuesday, after Christmas. For that season, Mr J.W.E. Bevin of Braunstone, Rutland joined David Bragg as the Joint Masters acting for the Committee. Peter Barrett was appointed as Kennel Huntsman in 1984, having been whipping-in. In 1992 Mr D (David) M Leather of Thorpe Langton, Market Harborough and Dr A.S. Jacks of Glooston, Market Harborough were appointed as a Joint Masters. Mrs D. Spree of Shearsby, Lutterworth, Leicestershire took on the post of Hon. Secretary in 1996. In 1999 Mrs E.A. Burton of Kilby, Leicestershire became a Joint Master and Mr D.A. (Charlie) Miller became Huntsman with Mr J.D. Royle as Deputy Huntsman. In 2001, the cap was raised from £6 to £10.

Captain R. Law's (1935–1939)

Captain Law formed his pack in 1935, probably with a draft from the Dalby Hall or the Eastington Park. He had further drafts from the Eastington Park and Viscount Tredegar. But the pack was disbanded, probably at the outbreak of the War in 1939.

Miss Barlow's (1937–1938)

Miss F. Barlow of Nottinghamshire had a pack in 1937–1938, but it included some 13in beagles.

Mr Mellor's (1938–1939)

Mr J.E. Mellor had hounds drafted from the Wick, Waltham, Eastington Park and Willoughby. Little is known about this Hunt. It was disbanded in 1939 and the hounds drafted to the Scalford Hall and Westerby.

** Castle Milk (1938–1962)*

In 1938 Mr A.R. (Rupert) J. Buchanan-Jardine of Castle Milk, Lockerbie, Dumfriesshire, imported five Basset Griffon Vendéen from France. He also had the draft of Westerby Warrior'32. These formed the basis of the Castle Milk which he formed as a private pack in 1939.

Rupert Buchanan-Jardine was the son of Sir John W. Buchanan-Jardine. Sir John hunted a country around Lockerbie with Foot Harriers and Beagles from 1921 until 1923. This country had remained unhunted then until 1939. Sir John was a well known expert on hounds and was acknowledged as having had great influences on the development of the Bloodhound and the Basset Hound in the UK. He was the author of the world renowned book of 1937 *Hounds of the World*. Sir John believed that the English Bloodhound had been developed in France from a 'Normandized' version of the St

Hubert Hound and that bassets had been developed from the Norman Hound which had, in turn, been developed along another route from the St. Hubert Hound. Sir John was an admirer of French 'Vénerie' in which hound work was the most important element in hunting, not riding. He is reputed to have said: '*I agree entirely . . . that a small pack produces better sport than a large one; I used to have some of my best hunts with seven or eight couple.*' He goes on to make the point that '*. . . working qualities such as nose and tongue are of more importance than conformation. I feel that this point is sometimes overlooked in this country where undue emphasis is placed on conformation.*'

Rupert Buchanan-Jardine was the Master and Huntsman of the pack and Mr A. Atkinson-Clark of Lockerbie was its first Hon. Secretary. The hounds initially consisted of 10 couple of rough coated bassets kennelled at Castle Milk. They met on Monday and Thursday. The country, hunted by the Dumfriesshire Foxhounds, was half open moorland with grass and plough. There were plenty of hares, '*usually too many*'. The hunt uniform was a green coat with a black collar and the evening dress was a green coat with a black collar and white facings.

In 1941 and 1942 he had two pure bred litters from the imported bitch, Flimsy (by the imports Blanco and Wildboy). From the second litter, he mated Wireless'42 to Blanco to produce another pure bred litter in 1944. In 1942 he also outcrossed one of the imports with a Westerby bitch, Languish'38. In 1946 the Castle Milk embarked on a major programme of outcrossing, first using a beagle, Statesman, thought to have come from either the Limbourne or the Clun Forest. Two of the resultant bitches, Saucebox'46 and Sapphire'46, were put to a Fell Hound, Caldbeck Fell Bloater'47, in 1949. One of the bitch offspring, Saintly'50, was then used (1954) with a harrier, Bowman'51 (By Modbury Worship, out of Cotley Bounty) and (1957 & 1958) with two beagles, Newcastle Jester'55 and Juggler'55.

The results of these cross-breedings had profound effects on the subsequent breeding in the Westerby and the Crowcombe in the late 1940s and the 1950s; and with the West Lodge in the beginning and the end of the 1950s. However, in 1962 the pack was disbanded. Some of the hounds may have been drafted to the West Lodge.

* *Scalford Hall (1940–1954)*

Following the outbreak of War in 1939 and his return to military duties, Eric Morrison dispersed the Westerby. Some went to Colonel George Colman OBE, TD, of the 9th Field Training Regiment, Royal Artillery in Yorkshire, who had been for many years Master of the Belvoir Foxhounds. They were kennelled at Scalford Hall, Melton Mowbray, Leicestershire. They hunted by kind permission of the Claro Beagles. In 1941 they took over the country previously hunted by the Thorp Satchville Beagles hunting over country of the Belvoir, Quorn and Cottesmore Foxhounds. Miss Burns-Hartopp whipped in. In 1954 the pack was disbanded and the hounds returned to the Westerby.

* *West Lodge Hare Hounds (1950-to present)*

In 1928 Sir Douglas Ritchie formed a private beagle pack which became a subscription pack in 1934. This pack was disbanded in 1941. In 1950 it was revived as the West Lodge Hare Hounds by Mr Lionel R. Woolner of Barnet, Hertfordshire who hunted the pack, with Mr D.G. Caroline of Potters Bar, Middlesex as Hon. Secretary.

The original pack consisted of fourteen couple of cross bred hounds, combining mainly Artésien-Normand and Griffon Vendéen basset with small harrier and beagle blood. They averaged 16in and many were rough-coated. The bassets were drafts from the Westerby, with some Grims blood lines.The harrier blood lines were from the

Caldbeck Fell, Dunston and from the Cambridgeshire. The beagle blood lines were from the Gellygaer and the Bolebroke. The Basset Griffon Vendéen blood came from the Castle Milk. Hounds were originally kennelled at Cotlands Wick, London Colney, Hertfordshire, owned by Lionel Woolner. Meets were held on Saturday and either Monday or Thursday. Subscriptions were three guineas, with a cap which was voluntary. The country lay mainly in Hertfordshire to the South of a line drawn from Elstree through Radlett, St. Albans, Hatfield and Hertford to Sawbridgeworth. There was no standard uniform, but the evening dress was a green waistcoat with yellow piping.

In 1951 Mr E. Shelley of West London joined Lionel Woolner as Joint Master and Huntsman. In 1952 Miss Joan Bennetts of Ridge, Hertfordshire took over a Hon. Secretary. Mr Shelley was succeeded as Joint Master in 1953 by Mr B.H. Sheppard of Arkley, Hertfordshire and the kennels were moved to the home of Mr John Evans at Arkley, Hertfordshire. John later hunted the BHC pack and became the first Master of the Albany. In 1954, Lionel Woolner became a founder member of the revived BHC and Mrs R. Plutte of Barnet, Hertfordshire became Hon. Secretary. Breeding had by then reduced the size of hounds to 15½in. In 1955 a Berkeley yellow collar was added to the uniform.

In 1958 Captain Raymond Brooks-Ward, a well known racing commentator of Waltham Abbey, Essex, took over as Joint Master and Huntsman with Lionel Woolner and in 1959 Mr Ted D. Dawson of Hatfield, Hertfordshire took the post of Hon. Secretary. The latter had been whipping-in since 1954. In 1960 additional country was acquired when the North Hertfordshire Beagles were disbanded. This was on either side of the Baldock-Royston road. In 1961, John Eden of Barnet, Hertfordshire became a third Joint Master.

The previous breeding policy continued but mainly using home bred lines with occasional blood lines from the Westerby. In 1966 a Petit Bleu de Gascogne bitch, Mongay Vaillante'59 was imported from Monsieur Mongay of Auc, Gers. She was mated to their own Striker'61. One dog and two bitches from the litter were subsequently used for breeding by the West Lodge. In 1966, Vaillante'59 was put to a KC registered Basset Hound, Stalwart Rebel'63. None of this litter appear to have been used for breeding by the West Lodge. One, Rosette'66, was drafted to the South Wales and another, Roulette'66, to the De Burgh. By 1965, there were fifteen-and-a-half couple in kennels. In 1966, Lionel Woolner died and Ted Dawson was appointed as Senior Master. Ted was replaced as Hon. Secretary in 1969 by H.N.C.(Tim) Denby-Wood of London N8.

But, at the end of the 1970 season the two Joint Masters resigned and John Powell-Williams, MBE of St Albans, Hertfordshire became the sole Master with Raymond Brooks-Ward holding the horn. In 1971 hunting was divided between Mr A. King-Cline of Woodside Park, North London and Tim Denby-Wood. In 1973 Mr H.O.J. Davies of Hertford became Joint Hon. Secretary with Tim Denby-Wood. The breeding continued using their own hounds, but some Westerby blood was used again in the early 1970s. In the latter half of the 1970s, KC registered Basset Hound blood lines were re-introduced from the Albany and from private breeders. In 1977 Mr A. King-Cline was appointed as a Joint Master.

1978 saw three Hon. Secretaries: Mr J. Kersey of Stansted, Mountfichet, Essex; Mr H. Murray-Stamp of Old Stevenage, Hertfordshire and Mr V. Richards of Welwyn, Hertfordshire. Mr A. Jones became Huntsman. The subscription was raised to £20 for an adult and £30 for a family, with a £1 cap. By 1980 the uniform was a black cap, green jacket with yellow facings, green socks and white breeches. In the following year the hounds were moved to kennels at Cambridge Road, Barton, Cambridgeshire. Neil J.F. Curtiss of Haverhill, Suffolk was appointed in 1983 as Joint Master and Huntsman. In 1985 Tim Denby-Wood shared the post of Hon. Secretary. The subscription was raised in 1985 to £25, family £49, with a cap of £2. In 1987 John E. Grande of Berkhampstead, Hertfordshire was appointed as a Joint Master. The post of Hon. Secretary was filled in 1988 by Mr C. Giggle of Stevenage, Hertfordshire.

The post of Hon. Secretary was taken over in 1992 by Mr and Mrs M.P. Willis of Benington, Hertfordshire and in the following year Mrs Gillian Willis of Haverhill, Suffolk became Joint Master with Mr William Burton of Great Dunmow, Essex. Jack Calder and then Paul Smith were Kennel Huntsmen. A Chairman, Mr T. Grimes, was appointed in 1997 and Tim Denby-Wood took on the Joint Mastership with Mr D. Sill as Huntsman. There were then twelve couple of hounds in the ownership of Mrs Willis. Richard Suter was appointed Hon. Secretary in 2000 and Martin Willis took on the post of Huntsman. It was agreed that the hounds were to be the property of the Committee. The cap was raised to £5.

In 2002 Mrs Gillian Willis resigned as Joint Master and was replaced by Martin Willis of Longstowe, Cambridgeshire who continued to hunt hounds. Sheila Denby-Wood, the wife of the Senior Master, Tim, took on the post of Hon. Secretary. The minimum subscription was set at £125. By 2004 the country had become difficult to hunt and the support had so diminished that it was decided to suspend hunting until alternative arrangements could be made. The country was loaned to the Albany for the 2004/5 Season.

* *Grims (1951–1964)*

Miss M.M. (Peggy) Keevil was born in 1910 in Surrey near Grim's Ditch. Her first dog was a mongrel, Potsford. After attending a school in Switzerland, she began to breed Scottish Terriers around 1931. She acquired her first Basset Hound in 1935, Dulcimara of Reynalton, from Mrs Nina Elms. This hound had been bred from two Walhampton hounds, Lynnewood and Nightshade, that Mrs Elms had purchased at the auction of the Walhampton when they were disbanded. This acquisition of a basset hound occurred as Miss Keevil trained in Kennel Management at the Bellmead Kennels at Egham, Surrey. Here Mrs Foster-Rawlin had kennelled her Potford hounds. Miss Keevil then moved to Inkpen, near Newbury, Berkshire and established the Grims kennels. In 1939 she bred her first Basset Hound, Grims Daisy'39 from her Dulcimara by Walhampton Medway (previously known as Merman'32). Thus began what was to be the survival of the Basset Hound in the UK through and after the Second World War.

At the outbreak of War, Lt. Col. Eric Morrison, the Master of the Westerby, lodged some Westerby hounds with Miss Keevil for the duration of the War, including Westerby Labram'38. Miss Keevil had also acquired Wick Welcome'35. In 1940, she mated Welcome to Westerby Marquis'38. From the litter of four hounds, two of them, the bitch Wishful'40 and the dog Worship'40, were to play leading parts in the formation of the Grims, although during 1941 to 1942, War conditions did not allow her to breed any hounds.

During 1943 and 1944 more Reynalton blood was introduced. In 1945 and 1947, Miss Keevil experimented with Bloodhound outcrosses. The first was with a dog, Reynalton Senator, a half bred Bloodhound x Basset Hound cross. The second was with a bitch, Reynalton Symbol, litter sister to Senator. Two of the resultant hounds, the bitch Grims Radium'44 and the dog, Grims Sermon'47, were later used by the Westerby, as well as being used in the Grims. One of the most influential progeny was

Grims with Miss Keevil circa 1953.

Grims Garrulous'49 and, from her, came Grims Gracious. The latter was acquired by Mrs Margaret Rawle and formed the basis of her Barnspark kennels. This hound became a KC Champion and her bloodlines are in many Basset Hound pedigrees throughout the world. At the 1958 Cruft's dog show, the Earl of Northesk said of her: *'A nice-headed bitch with deep set eyes showing haw, good neckline running into a long well-ribbed body. Very good front well-placed hocks and good tall carriage. Nice free mover.'*

In 1948 Miss Keevil went to France on a mission to find new blood to improve the then limited gene pool in England. Whilst she was fluent in French, she had great difficulty in locating and eventually buying stock. The Basset Hound had not been taken up in Europe and the Basset Artésien-Normand (BAN) had all but disappeared during the War, along with the other basset breeds. Those BAN that had survived or been re-created, were jealously guarded. Miss Keevil recounted to the author the difficulties she had in getting owners to let her see their hounds and how they initially hid their better specimens. The other problem was that none of them were hunted 'en force' and only some were used for hunting with a gun. But she did manage to import two BAN: the bitch, Cornemuse de Blendecques (Tayau x Vistule), from Monsieur Paul Leduc of Blendecques in the Pas de Calais and the dog, Ulema de Barly (Sans Souci de Bourceville x Querelle de Barly), from Monsieur Auguste Mallart of Barly in the Somme, who was the oldest established breeder of BAN. It was from the Mallart kennels that the Walhampton had acquired stock in 1921 via. Monsieur Verrier. Ulema, in particular, was an outstanding specimen, so much so that later leading French breeders decried his exportation. Ulema had a profound effect on Basset Hounds throughout the world, both in the show ring and in hunts. It was his influence in particular that produced the post-war English KC Standard for Basset Hounds. His instincts for hunting in a pack transformed the use of Basset Hounds for hunting in the UK and eventually led to the formation of several new hunts, as will be seen in this Chapter.

In 1951 Miss Keevil began to hunt privately on a regular basis on Wednesdays and Thursdays, as well as showing. The country she hunted was around Newbury and Hungerford in Berkshire in the Vine and part of the Tedworth and Craven Foxhound countries. There were then twelve couple of entered hounds. In 1952, Miss Keevil returned to France and came back with Aiglon des Mariettes (Taiaut de la Chee x Soupirante de Bourceville) from Mme. Raulin of Chermizy in the Aisne. This bitch did not have such quality as the other two BAN and played only a minor part in the development of the Grims.

By 1954, the Basset Hound had begun to revive in England, thanks to the efforts of Mrs Elms, Miss Keevil, Mrs Hodson, Mrs Grew and George Johnston and the improvements in quality resultant from the Bloodhound outcross and the importations from France. The BHC was refounded with Mr Alex McDonald as Chairman and Mrs Hodson as Secretary and Miss Keevil on the Committee. Major Jones-Stamp of the Craigcleuch and Lionel Woolner of the West Lodge were early members of the reformed BHC. In 1957 Mrs Hodson wrote of the BHC: *'We want to breed Bassets that retain the old characteristics but who are active and sound enough to hunt . . .'* This statement was reflected in the original Objectives of the new BHC. Indeed, during the period 1950 to 1964, the Grims won eleven out of forty-four Championships in the KC show rings and provided twenty-eight sires of Champions and twenty Dams of Champions. At the same time they were hunting.

Also in 1954, it was decided to adopt the US Standard for the Basset Hound as the International Standard. This required a heavier and lower set hound than that adopted by the KC in England. There is little doubt that this came about because the Basset Hound enjoyed greater popularity than in the rest of the world and had become a target for professional breeders. The BHC soon responded by deciding to import US stock and appointing Miss Keevil and Mrs Jagger to locate and purchase a hound. This they did, with difficulty and, in 1957, Lyn Mar Acres Dauntless was purchased by the BHC from Mrs Lynwood (Peg) Walton of Mount Holly, New Jersey. Dauntless was kennelled with the Grims. But he was not favoured by the show fraternity, although he was used by show breeders, partly because of the high costs of importation under the revised Quarantine Laws. In 1959 he was sold by the BHC to Miss Keevil, but never proved to be a useful hunter (he was nick named Doppy Joe!).

In 1958 the MBHA was revived by the efforts of Eric Morrison and Mrs Groom. They became the first Chairman and Hon. Secretary of the revived Association. The Grims registered with them and the Rules were revised to include the well established basset of the Westerby, the KC Basset Hound of the Grims and, by means of an Appendix, cross bred hounds.

By 1959, Miss Keevil had some fifty-five Basset Hounds, twenty sundry other dogs, Jacobs sheep, numerous cats, ducks, hens, bantams, geese, two monkeys and a pet fox. They were looked after by a full time kennel maid, Jean Osborne, and a part time handyman, Mr Stimpson. In 1960 Mr J. Hawes of Whitchurch, Hampshire became Huntsman and Hon. Secretary. By 1963, when the author first helped at the kennels, the number of Basset Hounds had risen to well over one hundred!

Sometime before 1956, the BHC decided to form a Working Branch to *'foster the hunting instinct in every Basset Hound.'* In 1959 the Grims assisted this venture. This was at a time when Miss Keevil began to reduce her interests in Basset Hounds as a result of her disagreement with the adoption of the US Standard. She carried on in the hope of changing this decision and by demonstrating the fitness of her type of Basset Hound via the Working Branch of the BHC. But in 1964 she also drafted many of her best working hounds to form the Fourshires. By 1969 her disagreements with the BHC reached a climax and she withdrew her hounds from participating with the BHC Working Branch. Several of her hounds were loaned to Mr David Mann as an encouragement to form the Leadon Vale. This marked the end of the Grims.

Miss Keevil moved on to breeding Pomeranians and with her immense knowledge of breeding was successful in recreating the chocolate variety. But she eventually closed her kennels and moved to East Dean, near Exmoor where she died in 1999.

* *Casewick (1948–1951)*
* *Crowcombe (1951–1955; 1957–1965)*

Major Thomas. F. Trollope-Bellew formed the pack in 1948 when he was living at Casewick, Lincolnshire. The original pack was formed from drafts from the Castle Milk, Scalford Hall and Westerby. One of the Westerby hounds Rodney'50 was by a Westerby dog Rennet'44 out of a Foxhound, Gellygaer Ringlet'48. They hunted the Cottesmore Foxhound country and part of the Belvoir and Fitzwilliam. In 1949 an experiment was made by using a beagle, Trinty Foot Marksman'44 on a Basset Hound, Captain Jones-Stamp's Dorothy'47. In 1951 and 1953 a beagle, Allendale Ranger'46, was used on Coquette'49.

In 1951 Major Trollope-Bellew moved to Crowcombe, Devon with his wife who became Joint Master and the Hunt was renamed. The area hunted was to the west side of the Quantocks, released to the Crowcombe by the Beacon Beagles in the West Somerset Foxhounds country and some of the West Somerset Vale. It is hilly country with high banks requiring speed, drive and stamina. Light coloured hounds were preferred as they could be easily seen.

In that year, further bloodlines were received from the Westerby by Redskin'50 The latter was by Westerby Rennet'44 again out of the foxhound Gellygaer Ringlet'48. In the following year, pure bred Basset Hound blood was introduced from the Grims, Marksman'52, by Grims Ulema de Barly'48, the imported Basset-Artésien-Normand, out of Kimblewick Musical'51, a pure bred KC registered Basset Hound. In the following year, Harrier blood was introduced from the Westerby by a litter by Dunster

Crowcombe at Old Cleeve, 1952. *Right* Maj. Trollope-Bellew, Master.

Gangway'48 out of Westerby Dairymaid'48. Dunston Gangway'48 was used again in 1951. Also Fell Hound blood was introduced in Crowcombe Sacrifice'50 by Calderbeck Fell Bloater'47 out of Castle Milk Sapphire'45.In 1952 Dunston Gangway'48 was used again on Crowcombe Rapture'49.

By 1954, hares had become very scarce and the pack had to be disbanded. However sufficient hares had returned by 1957 for the hunt to be revived, using drafts from the Westerby. One reason for the return of the hare was thought to have been the drastic reduction in rabbit numbers due to myxomatosis. The Westerby lines were continued through the early 1960s, plus the drafting of one bitch from the Grims, Crowcombe Belinda'61 by Grims Westward'55 out of Grims Chancy'57. In 1964 Belinda was put to a Harrier, Taunton Vale Victor'61. However, soon after this, the Trollope-Bellews gave up the hounds. Some were exported to the Tewksbury Foot Bassets in New Jersey, USA. Others were passed on to Mr Peter Butterfield who formed a pack of Harehounds based upon some hounds he had acquired in France. Major Trollope-Bellew and his two sons then started the Crowcombe Beagles.

Mr Jocelyn Lucas's (1914–1915)
** Sir Jocelyn Lucas's (1955–1958)*

Mr Jocelyn Lucas of Ilmer formed a pack of bassets just before the 1914 War began. But it had to be abandoned in 1915 following him being a prisoner of war in Germany. After the War, he became one of the leading breeders of Sealyham Terriers. He also bred other breeds, including hounds. Mr Lucas received a knighthood, won the Military Cross and became an MP after WWII.

In 1954 Sir Jocelyn became one of the founder members of the revived BHC. In 1955 he formed his second pack of bassets from drafts from the Westerby. He continued to use this line and an outcross to the Castle Milk until the pack was disbanded in 1958.

The Basset Hound Club Pack (1955–1972)

In 1955 the BHC Pack was revived. This was to advance the policy of the Club: *'the maintenance of the working utility as just as important as the quality of the show points. The policy is not to differentiate between the two: the Basset Hound should be handsome and useful.'* The Committee originally organised drag hunts and members were encouraged to take their hounds along. This was soon abandoned as it was found that hounds got bored of artificial trails. There were also organised walks with a view to getting individually owned hounds used to working together.

All this led to the idea of organising proper hunts, assessing the hunting ability of members hounds and awarding Working Certificates to those hounds who met basic criteria including: identifying and holding a line; giving tongue at appropriate times; and steadily hunting for at least two hours. However, there were no set requirements or scale of points in the judging, unlike the French Brevet de Chasse and the US Field Trials.

The nucleus of the pack were several couple of hounds loaned for the day by Miss M.M. Keevil from her Grims pack. The Master and Huntsman was Mr Alex J McDonald of West Molesey, Surrey, the President of the BHC, and the whips were Mr John Evans and his sons, Graham and Stephen of Arkley, Hertfordshire and the brothers Fulford-Dobson of Laleham, Middlesex (sons of Mrs Betty Fulford-Dobson, a breeder of Basset Hounds). The first Working Certificate was awarded 1959 to Ch. Grims Vapid owned Mrs Margaret Rawle of Allerford, Somerset. The first Secretary was Mrs Joan Cherrett, who was later succeeded by Miss Jane Blois. In the mid 1960s

The Basset Hound Club Pack at Great Linford, Bedfordshire, 1964. *Left* David Gandy, *centre* John Evans, *right* the tuthor.

John Evans took over as Master and Huntsman. The Hunt had no country of its own and met on most Saturdays during the season by invitation of landowners all over England, Scotland and Wales, hunting by permission of the local Masters of Hounds. It adopted the uniform of a fawn jacket with a yellow collar. Further encouragement to members to try their hounds was provided by the organisation of Regional Walks.

Mrs Rawle recounted to the author how Miss Keevil used to bring her hounds down to Porlock once a year for a meet of the BHC pack. One year they had a good hunt on the farms in Porlock Bay. The hunted hare was taken right round the bay and eventually took to the sea. At this point hounds were blown off and collected together. A little later, two fisherman caught up with the Hunt. Much to the horror of all, they produced a dead hare, explaining that they had seen it swim away, had gone out in a boat and caught it. They thought that the Hunt and the hounds would like it!

This Hunt changed its nature in 1969 when Miss Keevil withdrew her hounds as a result of a disagreement. Mr Evans then agreed to form a kennel and pack specifically for and financially supported by the Basset Hound Club. Hounds donated by members were kennelled with the West Lodge Hare Hounds at the home of Mr Evans at Arkley. In 1972 the Hunt completed registration of a country and was admitted as a Member of the MBHA under the name of the Albany. Details of this Hunt are given in a separate entry.

**North Warwickshire Hare Hounds (1955–1965)*

The North Warwickshire Hare Hounds were formed in 1951 by Mr Reg R. Wright of Coleshill, Warwickshire. They were originally five-and-a-half couple of pure bred Bloodhounds, owned by the Master and were kennelled at Grammar School Farm, Blythe Road, Coleshill, Warwickshire. They originally hunted the 'clean boot', i.e. the scent of a trail laid by a man who ran a course ahead of them. They were hunted on foot and occasionally mounted. Their country was loaned by the Warwickshire Beagles and hunted by permission of the Masters of the Atherston Foxhounds. They also hunted by invitation in other parts of the UK. The author recalls hunting with them and confirms their lovely cry. He also remembers Reg recalling how hounds inadvertently got into a Chapel. When asked what happened, he laconically said: *'They made a right mess of the pews!'*

An Hon. Secretary, Mr A.C.G. Richardson of Sutton Coldfield, Warwickshire, was appointed in 1955. Reg Wright developed another pack over the next few years, introducing beagle, Westerby and Casewick lines. Reg said that he liked the combination better than pure Bloodhound or Basset because he thought that the music was better. The pack was built up to fifteen couple in 1960 and reduced to twelve couple by 1965, but was disbanded sometime after this. Some of the hounds were drafted to the East Surrey Draghounds.

* *Kilspindie (1956–1969)*

Formed in 1956 as a private pack owned by the Master and Huntsman, Mr Humphrey ap Evans, MC of Pitfour Castle, Perth with the three or four couple of hounds drafted from the Westerby and kennelled at Kilspindie, Rait, Perthshire. There were no set days for meets. The uniform was buff with green facings. In 1959 his son, Adam Drummond, joined him as Master. Until 1966 hounds seem to have been home bred with some input from the Grims and some KC registered breeders. In 1966 hunting was suspended until the pack could be re-formed with imports of Basset Artésien-Normand from France. In 1968 the pack was described as being four couple of Artésien-Normand Bassets and Bleu de Gascogne, but no details have been found. In 1969 Adam Drummond was a Captain at Sandhurst and was hunting the Sandhurst Beagles. The hunt seems to have disbanded at the end of that year.

* *Herefordshire (1958–1966)*

In 1958 Mr Rex Hudson of Kilpeck, Herefordshire formed a private pack of twelve couple of hounds, based upon drafts from the Westerby and kennelled at The Firs, Kilpeck. They met by invitation on Saturday and occasional bye-days whilst negotiating a country. Hunting was in Herefordshire and, by invitation, in Gloucestershire, Worcestershire and Brecon. This was mainly grassland with some plough. The hunt coat was brown with a scarlet collar.

Mr, Hudson moved to Ross-on-Wye, Herefordshire in 1963. He was unable to hunt for two seasons, but continued to negotiate a country. But, in 1966 he had to disband the pack, although hoping to re-start it in the future.

Burgonet (1958–1975)

A private pack owned by Mr Norman and Mrs Winifred Burgess of Ringmer, Sussex in about 1958 and kennelled at their house. They also showed hounds. Winifred was Master and Norman was Huntsman. They hunted by invitation in East Sussex in the countries of the Brighton and Storrington Beagles and the Southdown Foxhounds. The pack was entirely composed of KC registered Basset Hounds. One hound was drafted to the Leadon Vale, Leadon Vale Julia'72. The pack was disbanded after the death of Norman Burgess.

* *Craigcleuch (1959–1968)*

Major S.D.B-Jones-Stamp of Craigleuch, Langholm, Dumfriesshire bred Basset Hounds from at least 1947 was a founder member of the revived BHC in 1954 and encouraged the formation of the Working Branch. In 1959 he formed a small private pack owned and hunted by himself with his wife as Hon. Secretary. The pack was composed of twelve couple of hounds drafted from the Grims and the Westerby, with a few KC registered Basset Hounds bred by the Barnspark kennel of Mrs Margaret Rawle of Porlock. They were kennelled both at Craigleuch and at the Queen Elizabeth Barracks, Strensham, York. The Kennel Huntsman was Private I.E. Foulkes. Initially meets were on Wednesdays in Yorkshire and Saturdays in Dumfriesshire. The countries hunted were the south-west of Dumfriesshire and around York, by permission of the Derwent Valley Beagles. The uniform was green corduroy with an evening dress of green corduroy, collar and waistcoat.

In 1962 the pack was moved to the kennels of the Derwent Valley Beagles. Mr David Kirk, Master of the Derwent Valley Beagles took the horn and became sole Master in 1964 and Mr C.W. Mann of York took over as Hon. Secretary. In 1965 a Ringwould blood line was introduced. In 1966 Mr Anthony Morris of Warthill, York became sole Master and Huntsman and the hounds were kennelled at his residence. The Hunt became a subscription pack with a single subscription of three guineas or five guineas for a family and a cap of five shillings. Meets were organised on most Saturdays with occasional bye-days. The country hunted lay in the North and East Ridings of Yorkshire, bounded in the West by the River Ouse, on the North by the York-Newcastle Railway line by the Howardian Hills to Malton and thence by the Malton-Scarborough Road thence by the Scarborough-Whitby Road, on the East by the coast, from Whitby to Bridlington, thence by the Bridlington-Driffield Road, thence by the Driffield-Market Weighton Road to the Market Weighton Road, and thence by the Canal to its confluence with the River Ouse. In 1967 a Hunt Club was formed with a minimum subscription of 5s., without cap for Hunt Club Members. The Hunt was disbanded in 1968, although the hunt uniform and evening dress were retained by the Derwent Valley Beagles to mark their association with the Pack.

** De Burgh (1960–1976)*
** De Burgh and North Essex Harehounds(1976 to present)*

Mr Robert E. Way, an antiquarian bookseller of Burrough Green, Newmarket formed and hunted the pack as a family concern at the end of the 1959–1960 season with his wife as Hon. Secretary. It was based upon gifts of seven couple of hounds from the Westerby and West Lodge Hare Hounds. They were kennelled at the Masters residence. Meets were arranged mainly on Saturday. There was a cap of two shillings for adults and one shilling for children. The country lay across the Cambridgeshire and Suffolk border and consisted largely of arable land, very heavy in parts, with considerable woodlands and also some fen. The uniform was a green corduroy coat and a green tie. Between 1963 and 1965 four litters were added from Westerby Rescue'58 by Westerby Ranger'57. In 1968 James V.E. Way took over as Huntsman from his father. In 1966 meets were expanded to Wednesday and Saturday as could be arranged.

At the end of the 1970–1971 season Robert Way decided to retire and relinquish the pack. Many of the hounds were drafted to other packs. Fortunately, Mr John S. Humphrey of Debden Green, Saffron Walden, Essex took over the remaining pack, became Master and Huntsman and kennelled them at his farm. The South Wales, Leadon Vale and Huckworthy drafted hounds and the pack was reconstructed by breeding with these. A green collar was added to the uniform coat. Meet days changed to Tuesday and Saturday. In 1972 Miss S. Norwak of Thaxted, Essex took on the post of Hon. Secretary. Extensive breeding was undertaken, mainly using Leadon Vale

De Burgh and North Essex with Mrs Edna Philp, Master and Huntsman, 2004.

drafts and West Lodge blood lines. By 1973 there were ten-and-a-half couple in kennels. Meets reverted to Saturdays and occasional bye days. In 1975 a harrier outcross was used from the dog, Cambridgeshire Statesman'71.

At the end of the 1975–1976 season the North Essex Foot Hunt Club was amalgamated with the De Burgh and part of the country hunted by the North Essex Foot Beagles, until its cessation, was incorporated into the De Burgh country. Mr Michael W. Mann, MC, MA, who had been Master of the North Essex Foot Beagles since 1964, of Tilty, Great Dunmow, Essex became Hon. Secretary. The name of the hunt was changed to the De Burgh and North Essex Hare Hounds. Subscriptions rose to eight guineas with a cap of fifty pence.

In 1982 the subscriptions were raised to £19 and £10 for juniors and the cap to £2. In 1987 Mrs H. Robson of Hatfield Broadoak, Bishops Stortford, Hertfordshire took on the post of Hon. Secretary. By 1988 there were twelve couple of English Bassets owned by the Master in kennels. The subscriptions had then been raised to £24 and £35 for a family. In 1990 the Master moved to Radwinter, Saffron Walden, Suffolk and the kennels were moved there. Subscriptions were raised to £28 and £40 for a family.

For the first time in 1992 a Joint Master, Peter Basssett of Thaxted, Essex, was appointed with John Humphrey. Peter had whipped in since 1988. John Townrow of Wethersfield, Braintree, Essex was appointed Joint Master in 1995. In the following year Mrs Edna Philp took on the hunting from John Humphrey, following his move to France. The hounds went to livery at the kennels of the East Suffolk Foxhounds at Earls Colne. The subscriptions had to be raised substantially to £100 single, £150 family and the cap to £4.

John Humphrey was tragically killed in a car accident in France in 1997. Following the retirement of both the other Joint Masters, Mrs Edna Philp of Castle Hedingham, Essex, was appointed as sole Master and continued hunting hounds. At the same time, Mrs J. Burton of Dunmow, Essex took on the post of Hon. Secretary. Cost increases meant raising the subscription to £120 and £175 family and the cap to £5 and again in 2000 to £130 and £185 family. In 2000 Peter Thomas of Radwinter, Saffron Walden joined Edna as Joint Master.

Ringwould (1961–1964)

In 1946 Mr William Marsh of Ringwould, Deal, Kent kennelled and became Joint Master of the R.A. (Dover) Beagles, which then became the R.A. (Ringwould) Beagles. He later exchanged them for Basset Hounds, forming a private pack with himself as sole Master. In about 1962 he changed these for a draft of bassets from the Westerby as he regarded these hounds as being better suited to plough. The pack of ten couple was hunted by Ivor Bianchi. They met on Saturday. The uniform was green. The country lay between Dover and Sandwich. It was open, undulating country, principally arable. The Hunt was disbanded in 1964. Hounds may have been returned to the Westerby.

** East Suffolk(1961–1967)*

A private pack established in 1961 by Mr and Mrs C.G.L. Marriott of Saxmundham, Suffolk to hunt over their land and the properties of neighbours and friends. They received drafts from the Westerby, West Lodge and Herefordshire. The ten couple of hounds were kennelled at their farm. There are no fixed days for meeting in order to avoid clashing with shooting dates and the meets of local packs of hounds. There was no subscription. The pack was disbanded in 1967. Some hounds appear to have been drafted to the Oaston and to the Westerby.

** Oaston (1963–1975)*

The hunt was formed in 1963 by the Master and Huntsman, Mr C.H. Frisby of Nuneaton, Warwickshire with his wife and Mr T. Smith of Nuneaton, Warwickshire as Joint Secretaries. They had acquired a KC registered Basset Hound by 1960. Until 1965 they built up their pack from more KC registered hounds and a beagle bitch, North Warwickshire Wistful'59. Their hounds were kennelled at Oaston Fields, Nuneaton. Meets were on Saturday with occasional bye-days. The country lay in Warwickshire and Leicestershire and was hunted by kind consent of the North Warwickshire and the Atherstone Foxhounds. It was half plough and half grass.

In 1964 Mr E. Ball took over the Mastership and Mr R.H.A. Milligan of Coundon, Coventry became Hon. Secretary. In 1965 Mr T. Twigger was appointed as Huntsman. By then there were sixteen-and-a-half couple in kennels. From 1966 the hounds were changed to English bassets and the kennels were re-located to Spring Hill, Arley, near Nuneaton and then, in 1967, to Houndsmill Lane, Allesley, near Coventry. Hounds had returned to fourteen couple, the property of the Hunt. In 1968 Mr C.M. Faulkes took over the Joint Mastership with Mr T. Twigger.

In 1971 Mr R.H.C. Pickering of Burwell, Leicestershire and Mr Don A. Peacock of Barbage, Leicestershire took on the Joint Mastership, with Mrs R.H.C. Pickering as Hon. Secretary. Don Peacock hunted hounds that season and Mr Pickering the following season. In 1972 Mrs Pickering became a Joint Master with Mr D.R. Hands of Burwell, Leicestershire. A family subscription was £5.25 and a single subscription £3.15, with a cap of 25p. In 1971 to 1973 beagle blood was introduced using the stallion hounds Chilmark Farrier'63 and Stowe Padlock'66 and the bitch Newcastle and District Whiterose'70. But none of the subsequent progeny seems to have been used for breeding. Unfortunately, the country was becoming difficult to hunt, as a result of building and motorways. The hunt was finally disbanded in 1975 and the hounds drafted to the Westerby.

* *Fourshires (1963–1980; 1988 to present)*
* *West Oxfordshire (1980–1988)*

Between 1963 and 1968, Miss Keevil of the Grims gave Mr Derek Meredith of Chipping Norton, Oxfordshire over twelve couple of hounds to form a pack, the Fourshires, to succeed the Grims. These became the property of the Committee. The name of the Hunt came from the nearby Four Shires stone marking the boundary of Oxfordshire, Warwickshire, Gloucestershire and Worcestershire. Mr Matthew McDermott of Moreton-in-the-Marsh, Gloucestershire became Joint Master with Derek Meredith for the 1964–1965 season. Mrs, now Lady, Higgs of Great Enstone, Oxfordshire took the post of Hon. Secretary. Hounds were kennelled at Derek Meredith's farm and the Kennel Huntsman was Mr R. Irvine. Meets were on Saturday and the subscription was set at two guineas and seven guineas for a family with a cap of five shillings. The Hunt has never had any country of its own, but meets by invitation in Worcestershire, Warwickshire, Gloucestershire and Oxfordshire. The hunt uniform is a fawn jacket with a green collar.

Mrs M.S. Argles of Church Enstone, Oxfordshire succeeded Matthew McDermott as Joint Master in 1966. In 1970 Derek Meredith was joined by Mr David A. Lloyd of Moreton-in-Marsh, Gloucestershire as Acting Joint Master, due to problems in running the Hunt. Mr M.J. Jones was appointed Kennel Huntsman. He was succeeded in 1972 by Arthur Rawlings. Breeding continued along the Grims lines with occasional use of KC registered hounds of private breeders. In 1975 Mr John H. Lloyd of

Fourshires, circa 1967.

Dagensford, Oxfordshire was appointed Master with Derek Lloyd retiring. In 1978 John Lloyd hunted the hounds with Neil James. In 1979 they decided to introduce some Westerby blood lines and Mr R. Gardener of Clifton, Oxfordshire became Joint Master.

In 1980 the name of the hunt was changed to the West Oxfordshire. The ten couple of bassets were moved to kennels at the home of John Lloyd. Mr B.T. Humphries of Middle Barton, Oxfordshire became Hon. Secretary and Mr R. Dixon began hunting hounds. The subscriptions were raised to £10, £15 for a family and a 50p. cap. John Lloyd moved in 1982 to Oddington, Stow-on-the-Wold, Gloucestershire. C.S. Hillam became Kennel Huntsman in the following year. Mr Richard Schuster of Middle Barton, Oxfordshire became Joint Master in 1984. and Mr D. Gaylord hunted hounds. Subscriptions were raised to £20, £30 for a family and a £2 cap. Lady Higgs became Chairman in 1987.

In 1988 the Hunt reverted to the name Fourshires and Mrs J. Schuster of Morton, Oxfordshire became Hon. Secretary and Nigel Cunningham took on the hunting. The subscription was raised again to £60. In 1990, Boyce Keeling was appointed to hunt hounds, having previously hunted the Warwickshire Beagles. But at the end of the 1990/91 season, Derek Meredith and Richard Schuster resigned. For a time it looked as though the Hunt would have to be disbanded and plans were made to send some of the hounds to the USA.

Fortunately, Lady Higgs and Mr Charles Cottrell-Dormer, of Morton-in-the-Marsh, Gloucestershire agreed to become the new Joint Masters. At the same time the hounds were put to livery at the kennels of the Christ Church and Farley Hill Beagles at Worminghall Road, Stanton St John, Oxfordshire under the Kennel Huntsman, Les Atkinson. Roy Dixon took on the hunting. The Hon. Secretaryship moved to Mrs E. Parkhurst of Steeple Aston, Oxfordshire, who also took on the Hon. Secretaryship of the Supporters Club. The subscriptions became discretionary and the cap raised to £5. The Hon. Secretaryship of the Supporters Club later changed to Dr Angela Smith of Steeple-Aston, Oxfordshire. New country was received on loan from the Dummer Beagles.

In 1995 Dr John Cordingley of Adderbury, Oxfordshire was appointed as a Joint Master. Michael Smith became Kennel Huntsman in 1996. He was succeeded by Barry Fews in 1998. In that year Andy Coupe of Bicester, Banbury, Oxfordshire was appointed as Joint Master, having hunted hounds since 1995. By 2000 there were twenty couple of hounds of mixed English and Anglo-French bassets. Hunting took place on some Tuesdays, as well as Saturdays. In 1999 Andy Coupe handed over the hunting to Peter Sherwood, who had been whipping in since 1977, and retired as Joint Master in the following year. By 2002, there were sixteen couple of hounds. In 2004 Mrs Joan Murrall of Cassington, Witney Oxfordshire became Hon. Secretary. Subscriptions were £100 with a family at £150 and a cap of £5.

Basset Hound Club of Ireland (1966–1989)

The Basset Hound Club of Ireland was formed in 1966 with objectives which included promoting hunting of Basset Hounds. Hunting took place intermittently from 1970 to 1976. In the following year Mr Darby Kennedy was appointed as Master and hunting took place regularly throughout the season on Sundays. Darby was succeeded as Master by Denis O'Connor in 1978. By 1980 a country had been established in co. Kildare and co. Meath consisting of farmland, hills and bog. About that time Mr Dennis P. Dowdall of Dundrum, Dublin took over as Master, Huntsman and Hon. Secretary. The subscription was £2 for a family with a cap of 30p per person or 50p for a family. The Hunt was still in existence in 1989.

* *South Wales (1966–1996) Vale of Glamorgan (1996–1998)*

The Hunt was formed in the latter part of the 1966 season by the Joint Masters: Lady Treherne, JP, OBE of Coedarhydgln, near Cardiff and Col. Norman P. Thomas, MBE TD DL of Llantwit Major, Glamorgan, who were also the Joint Hon. Secretaries. The hounds were drafted from the Westerby and the De Burgh. The Joint Masters were soon joined by Mr George Vaughan of St Mary Hill, Glamorgan and Mr Nicholas Harby of Bridgend, Glamorgan. Tom Keen was appointed as Huntsman. Meets were on Saturday with occasional bye-days. There was no subscription, but a cap of 2s.6d. The uniform was a brown coat with a yellow collar. The country hunted was South Glamorgan from Cardiff to Pyle and from Pontypridd to the Bristol Channel. It was hunted by kind consent of the Glamorgan and Pentyrch Foxhounds, later also the Banwen Miners Foxhounds. It was very varied from good arable land in the south to mountain moor in the north.

In 1969 Nicholas Harby retired as Joint Master. In that year and in 1970 the pack was increased by generous drafts from the Westerby and the De Burgh and Tom Keen was appointed as a Joint Master. In 1973 the kennels were moved to Cottrell St. Nicholas, near Cardiff, when there were ten couple of hounds. Mr Idawl E Symonds, J.P. of Dinas, Powys was appointed as Joint Master on the retirement of Lt. Col. Thomas. The pack was gradually built up to thirteen couple by 1978. In 1978 Mr Charles E. Harrison, JP. of Wenvoe, near Cardiff took over as Joint Master from George Vaughan. Mrs B.V. Harrison became Hon. Secretary in 1980 and Mr S. Taylor hunted hounds. He was succeeded in 1982 by Mrs J. Studley. Mrs Harrison became a Joint Master in 1985. John Roberts, who had been whipping-in, became Huntsman in 1989. In 1993 Mr S.A. Wenham of Cowbridge, Glamorgan was appointed as a Joint Master.

In 1996 Mrs Jane Rees of Newton Cowbridge, South Glamorgan became a Joint Master. But, in the middle of the 1996–1997 season, three Joint Masters resigned. Mrs Rees decided to carry on as sole Master and renamed the Hunt the Vale of Glamorgan

South Wales, 1988. Mr Clive Rees, Joint Master and Huntsman.

Basset Hounds as a private pack. There were fifteen couple of pure-bred Basset Hounds *'of the sort perceived by Lady Rowena Treherne during her long Mastership, rather than the crossbred hounds preferred by the South Wales since 1983.'* The hounds kennelled by Mrs Rees at her home. They were hunted by Clive Jeffrey Rees of Swansea, who also acted as Hon. Secretary, with other members of the Rees family whipping-in. There was no subscription and the cap was voluntary. The country hunted was the whole of the Vale of Glamorgan by kind permission of the Glamorgan, Llangeinor and Pentych Foxhounds, plus the Pentych's hill country to the west of the River Taff. Also hunted by permission of the Banwen Miners' Foxhounds was the whole of west Glamorgan comprising the Gower peninsular and the hills surrounding the Newton and Swansea Valleys Hunts. The latter part of the 1997 season was reported as finding *'an exceptional number of hares in the Valley country and hunting them with great passion, drive and music.'* The Vale of Glamorgan was disbanded in 1998.

* *Leadon Vale (1967-to present)*

At the Evesham Horse Show in 1958, David Mann saw his first Basset Hound, Maybush Modesty. As a result, he acquired Grims Wild Air. He then visited the Grims kennels and obtained Grims Fidget'60 and Grims Wedlock'62. From the latter he had forty whelps from three litters. His first wife, Barbara, began to show and the Spurbridge Kennels were formed at Cobbs Cross, Kings Green, Berrow, near Malvern, Worcestershire, near the Ledbury Foxhound Kennels.

Leadon Vale, 1968. Foreground, left: Mr M.P. Price; centre: David Mann, Master & Huntsman; right: Ray Tucker, whip. Mrs Barbara Mann is behind and to left of Master with Mrs Price. Ray Gould, whip, is behind Mr Tucker. Mr Ernie Mansell, Joint Master, at rear.

As a result and with the encouragement of Miss Keevil, in 1967 he formed and hunted the Leadon Vale. His first Joint Master was Mr Ernest (Ernie) Mansell of Churchdown, near Gloucester. The Hon. Secretary was Mr John Keen of Pendock, near Stoughton, Gloucestershire. The first President was Miss Rosemary Philipson-Stowe. Subscriptions were set at three guineas single and five guineas family with a cap of five shillings. The hounds were the property of David Mann and kennelled at Cobbs Cross. Meets were on Saturday and occasional Wednesdays. One of the first meets was at the farm of Nancy and Walter Biddlecombe, the parents of Terry Biddlecombe who went on to become the leading Hunt Jockey. The country lies in the Cotswold Vale Farmers Hunt, the Berkeley and the Ledbury Foxhound countries, bounded by the Ross Harriers, Wyre Forest, Warwickshire, Dummer, Clifton Foot, Monmothshire and Royal Agriculture College Beagles, in the vale of the River Leadon and Gloucestershire, and between the Malvern Hills and the Forest of Dean. The uniform is a buff jacket with blue facings and blue stockings and, the coat for Masters and evening, blue with buff facings. Originally, a blue hard hat was worn, later changed to a blue cap.

During the rest of the 1960s and the early 1970s the pack was built up by a draft of nine-and-a-half couple from the Grims in 1968 and use of other KC registered Basset Hounds of private owners. The emphasis was improvement of feet and fronts. There were problems, as David Mann once explained: '*the pack leader from the Grims, Drummer, nearly started WW3 by leading off the joint pack whilst on exercise in pursuit of a French (naturally) onion-seller. The hunt stopped either because the bicycle broke a speed record or "scent gave out!"*' Unfortunately, David Mann contracted salmonella in 1970 and was hospitalised as a result of a heart attack. But, true to form, he managed to convince the staff that a visit of some of his hounds to his bed in hospital would speed his recovery! Fortunately the supporters were able to keep the hunting going, notably with Greg Tustin and David Philpotts hunting on Saturdays and Harry Bainbridge during the week.

In 1971 Terry G. Mayo of Upton St Leonards, Gloucestershire and Brian E. Wilson of Horsell, Surrey succeeded Ernie Mansell as Joint Masters with David Mann. Terry had been whipping in and Brian had been helping Miss Keevil for some years. By then there were over fifteen couple in kennels. In 1974, Brian had to relinquish his Mastership because the rationing of petrol did not allow him to travel from Surrey. Messrs. R.S. Smith of Chellerton, Gloucestershire and David Taylor of Churchdown, Gloucestershire took over as Joint Masters. There were then twenty couple in kennels.

Throughout the 1970s the Leadon were able to use their own hounds for breeding, thanks to the wide variety of breeding lines which they had. In 1975 Mr M.W. Tytherleigh became Joint Master. In 1978 David Taylor took over the hunting of hounds and Mr C.J. Welch of Lydney, Gloucestershire became Joint Master. In 1979 David Mann handed over the hunting to Greg I. Tustin, who was appointed as Joint Master.

In 1980 Miss Keevil gave up the Grims kennels, near Newbury and moved to East Dean in Devon. By then she was not well. To look after her and because his own health now prevented him from looking after hounds, David Mann and his wife moved down to Devon. The seventeen couple were moved into livery at the Croome Foxhound kennels. Fortunately, Mr David K. Oliver of Pershore, Worcestershire was able to take on both a Joint Mastership and the hunting, having had a number of years with the Wyre Forest Beagles. The ownership of the hounds remained with Mr and Mrs Mann. David Philpotts of Gadley, Malvern, Herefordshire became Hon. Secretary, having been whipping in from 1979. To finance keeping the hounds at livery, the subscription was raised to £10 with a £1 cap. Membership was by invitation. Bye days changed to Monday and Thursday during school holidays as David Oliver was a Headmaster. The policy of the Hunt remained to *'maintain a pure bred pack of French Bassets, from which the worst faults of the breed had been eliminated by careful breeding'*. The breed that was being referred to were a basset based upon the French Basset Artésien-Normand.

In 1984 David Mann gave ownership of the hounds to the Hunt Committee. By 1986 the subscriptions rose again to a minimum of £45, £60 for families, £15 for juniors and pensioners, with field money of £1 and a visitors cap of £2. Mr David Philpotts was appointed as Joint Master by the Committee in 1988. By 1993 costs required subscriptions to be further increased to a minimum of £60, £80 for families, £25 for students and pensioners, with field money of £2, visitors cap £3.

In 1994 the Hunt decided that it would become a Committee Hunt and Mr Philip Hocking of Snowshill, Broadway, Worcestershire became Chairman. Mr Anthony Greenwood of Grafton, Tewkesbury, Gloucestershire and Mr Charlie H. Grinnall of Chipping Camden, Gloucestershire. were appointed as Joint Masters and Charlie took on the hunting. A new Constitution was adopted which enshrined the original policy of breeding hounds of the Basset Artésien-Normand characteristics. In 1996 Barry Read took over the hunting as replacement for Charlie. Ted Burston was appointed as Hon. Secretary. In 1997 Ted became Treasurer and the post of Hon. Secretary was taken by Bob Perry of Bromsgrove, Worcestershire. Mrs M P Major, a Joint Master of the Modbury Harriers, agreed to become a Joint Master. In the same year, the hunting passed to Steven Evans of Lower Broadheath, Worcestershire. Steven had previously hunted mink hounds. He became Joint Master in 1999 and Mrs Penny Plath of Bredon Pershore, Worcestershire was appointed as Hon. Secretary in replacement of Bob Perry. There were twenty couple of hounds in kennels in this year.

In 2000 Anthony Greenwood retired as Joint Master and took the post of Chairman on the resignation of Philip Hocking. Michael Whitehead of Spetchley, Worcestershire who had been whipping-in since 1994, became Joint Master. Rising costs forced the Committee to raise subscriptions to £80 with £110 for a family or £50 for pensioners and students, with a £5 cap. In 2001, Mrs Major retired as a Joint Master. In 2004 Penny Plath retired from the post of Hon. Secretary and Mrs R. Chichester of Worcester took on the post. In 2004 Mr Charles Pickles was appointed as Chairman. He had been Master of the Shrivenham Beagles.

Stevenstone (1968–1972)

The Hunt was formed by the Master and Huntsman, Mr F.T. Sumner of Torrington Station, North Devon, in 1968 with seven couple of Westerby type bassets. They met on Friday. The uniform was a green coat and green stockings. They hunted the Stevenstone Foxhound country. The Hunt appears to have been disbanded in 1972.

Melancthon(1968–2002)

In the early 1960s Mrs W.M. Aspin of Knutsford, Cheshire purchased her first Basset Hound, Brockhampton Restless, from Mr Gerald Dakin of Preston, Lancashire. She went on to breed them and became involved with the Working Branch of the BHC. As this involved much travelling, she determined to form a Working Branch in the North West. Having obtained permission by the Masters of the Cheshire Forest Foxhounds and bordering Beagles, the Melancthon began to hunt in 1968 with Mrs Aspin's hounds and some owned by BHC members in the North West, all KC registered Basset Hounds. The Hunt uniform was a green jacket with a royal blue collar, white breeches,

Melancthon Basset Hounds.

blue socks and a black cap. Meets were on Saturdays. Having a small country, invitation meets were held in Anglesey (where Mrs Aspin had another house), Yorkshire, Montgomeryshire and Shropshire. Gradually her pack was built up to 8 couple of hounds. Former Huntsman have included Bob Dixon, Dr Anton Aspin and Graham Browne. Unfortunately, Mrs Aspin's health failed and the country could not be kept open after the Foot & Mouth epidemic of 2001. The Pack has been reduced to 2 ½ with the intention of resuming in the future.

* *Mid-Down (1968–1972) Ross-shire Hare Hounds (1972–1973) Petre Uchaf Harehounds (1973–1982) Hadfar Harehounds (1982–1984)*

The Mid-Down was established as a private pack in 1968 by Dr D.Garfield Rees, MB, ChB of Ballynahinch, Co. Down, Northern Ireland, who hunted them. It consisted of four-and-a-half couple of drafts from the Oaston and the De Burgh, together with some Irish KC registered Basset Hounds. They were kennelled at The Bungalow, Crossgar Road, Ballynahinch. Meets were on Thursday and Saturday, followed by invitation of the Master, which automatically included landowners and the members of the County Down Staghounds, and adjacent Foxhounds, Harriers and Beagle Packs. The uniform was a navy blue jacket and tie and navy blue stockings. The country was formerly hunted by the Fermac Beagles and mostly lay between Hills-boro, Dromore and Ballynahinch, within the territory of the County Down Staghounds.

In 1972 Dr Rees moved from Ireland to Evanton, Ross-shire in Scotland and re-established the Hunt as the Ross-shire Hare Hounds. It consisted then of four couple of Westerby type bassets and Bleu de Gascogne from the Mid-Down. It was a private pack followed by invitation. The uniform was a navy blue jacket and stockings. The country hunted was situated in Easter Ross, the territory included an area of arable farmland in the Eastern half. The rest was open moorland and mountain. Hares were plentiful.

In 1973 Dr Rees moved from Scotland to Wales at Petre Uchaf, Kelin Crai, Brecon,

Powys and the Hunt became the Petre Uchaf Harehounds. There were then were seven couple Bleu de Gasconge and Harrier-Basset crosses of Westerby origin, 16 to 19in. They were said to hunt relatively slowly but with great accuracy and music. The Hon. Secretary was Mrs J. May of Postycray, Brecon. Meets were on Tuesday and Saturday and were occasionally mounted. Subscriptions were taken and the cap was £1. The uniform was a green coat with a black collar. The country was the hills in West Breconshire, hunted by the Sennybridge Foxhounds. In 1975 Mr David Evans of Maesteg, Glamorgan became Joint Master.

Dr Rees moved in 1982 to Trecastle, Brecon with David Evans remaining as Joint Master.The Hunt was renamed the Hyndfar Harehounds. Mrs J. May of Tulgarth, Brecon became Hon. Secretary. They continued to hunt the same country. The Hunt apparently disbanded about 1984.

* *Huckworthy (1969-2004)*

The Huckworthy were formed as a private pack in 1969 by Major Cecil Hall Parlby and his wife, Mrs Audrey Parlby at their home in Charlton Horethorne , near Sherborne in Dorset. Mrs Parlby had had a long association with bassets. She was the great niece of Arthur Croxton-Smith, one of the leading breeders of bassets at the turn of the twentieth century. She obtained her first basset from Mrs Elms in 1934, Juno of Reynalton (132S) and went on to breed Basset Hounds. She became more and more interested in producing a type which could hunt. This involved a small amount of outcrossing with bassets from other packs.

Cecil's cousins, Roger and Philip Mott had been beagling for many years and offered to hunt a pack if a country could be found. A country was registered in 1969 and Dr Roger Mott, was the first Huntsman. The Huckworthy originally had ten couple of pure-bred Basset Hounds, mainly bred from Mrs Parlby's own stock. The country lay within the Mendip Farmers Hunt, between the Rivers Parrett and Brue, mainly on the Polden Hills and was extended in 1974 to include much of the Blackmore Vale

Huckworthy with Joint Master and Huntsman, Mr Philip Mott, QC.

Foxhound country. The uniform was a green coat with a tan collar, tan cap and waistcoat, and green stockings. Meets were on Saturday with occasional bye-days. The cap was 2s.6d.

Following Major Parlby's death in 1971, Major C.P.T. Rebbeck of Pensford, Bristol took over the Joint Mastership in 1972. In 1973 subscriptions were introduced and the Hon. Secretary was Mrs Caroline Rebbeck. In 1973 Mr Philip C. Mott of Taunton, Somerset took over the Joint Mastership and hunted hounds, having been whipping-in since their formation. In 1974 he was joined in the hunting by Mr M. Rickard who had been whipping-in previously. In 1977 the cap was raised to £1, with children at 30p. In 1979 Mr A.T. MacCaw was appointed Huntsman. In the following year Mr D. Schreiber of Yeovil, Somerset joined Mrs Parlby and Philip as Joint Master on the retirement of Major Rebbeck. In 1981, the Huntsman, Mr A.T. MacCaw of Sherborne, Somerset was appointed Joint Master, allowing hunting to become two days a week on Tuesdays and Saturdays. In 1986 Mr A.S. Head of Queens Camel, Yeovil, Somerset took on the post of Hon. Secretary and Mr MacCaw retired as Joint Master. In 1988 there were twelve couple of hounds in kennels. In 1990 Mr M. Hicks took over as Huntsman. For much of this period, boys from the nearby Sherborne School were encouraged to come out to learn about hunting and to carry a whip to the hounds. This was in exchange for a large tea before they returned to school.

In 2001 David Hartless was appointed as Kennel Man. However, David's lack of experience of hunting and Philip's work as a QC, Colonel John Parkes OBE of Corton Denham, Dorset was appointed as a Joint Master to assist him and to hunt hounds in his absence. The Hunt also organised local events to recruit new members, especially children.In 2002 David Hartless had gained sufficient experience to become Kennel Huntsman. In 2003, two-and-a-half couple of hounds were drafted to La Ciguela, a hunt formed of Basset Hounds hunting hare by the Master, Senor Jose Manuel Jimenez of La Rioja, Spain.

Following Mrs Parlby's death early in 2004, the pack had to be disbanded, but the country was kept open by loaning it to the Park Beagles. Three-and-a-half couple were drafted to the East Lincolnshire, three couple to the De Burgh, one-and-a-half couple to the Albany and a further two couple to La Ciguela. The remaining hounds were privately re-homed as pets, with the assistance of Basset Hound Rescue Welfare.

Test Valley (1969–1975)

Formed and hunted in 1969 by Rory Dicker of South Warnborough, Hampshire.The Hon. Secretary was Miss D. Van Der Kiste of Salisbury, Wiltshire. The foundation hounds were five-and-a-half couple from the Westerby. Initially, they were kennelled at Embley Park, Romsey and later at Bensgrove Farm, Reading where the Farley Hill Beagles were kennelled. The country was on loan from the New Forest Beagles in a triangle outside the Forest boundary with Salisbury, Winchester, and Romsey forming the boundary. Meets were held on Thursdays until the end of the shooting season with some Saturday meets added. Invitation weeks were held in Devon and Dumfriesshire. Adjacent hunts were Palmer Milburn to the north, Meon Valley to the east, New Forest to the south and Pimpernel (Royal Signals) to the west. This was a private pack with no subscription but a cap of 25p was taken. Hunt uniform was a black coat with fawn corduroy collar, breeches, and bottle green flat cap. Evening dress – black coat, fawn collar and yellow silk facings.

In later years, Rory introduced beagles to the pack. In 1972 he moved to Lincolnshire and registered as the East Lincolnshire, hunting the old Skegness Beagle

Test Valley with Master and Huntsman, Mr Rory Dicker, leaving original kennels at Embley Park near Romsey, Hampshire.

country. Hounds were kennelled at Clough Farm, Croft, Skegness. Mr David Farrant of Revesby became Hon. Secretary until 1974 when Mr M.J. Elestron of Market Rasen, Lincolnshire took the post. In 1975 Rory moved to Co. Tipperary, Ireland where he took some hounds and amalgamated with the Kilfeacle Beagles. The remaining bassets were presented to the East Lincolnshire Harehounds Committee.

** Albany (1972-to present)*

In 1972 the Basset Hound Club Pack became formerly established with a country and registered with the MBHA. It took the name of Albany in recognition of the fact that it hunted all over England to encourage members of the BHC to take an active interest in the working qualities of Basset Hounds. The Committee appointed as Acting Masters Mr E. John Evans of Arkly, Barnet, Hertfordshire, who had hunted the BHC Pack since 1965, and Mr Tim D. Thomas of Stamford, Lincolnshire. Miss Jane Blois of London was Hon. Secretary, a post which she had held for many years with the BHC Pack. Ten-and-a-half couple of KC registered Basset Hounds were kennelled at Mr Evans residence and were owned by the BHC. Meets took place on Saturday and occasional bye days. There was a voluntary subscription and a cap of 25p. The uniform of the BHC Pack, snuff jacket with gold collar, was retained. The registered country is situated in the Cottesmore Foxhounds country and comprises East Rutland and South Leicestershire. It extends from Melton Mowbray to Oakham to the west; Oakham to Spalding to the east; Bourne to Colsterworth to the north. The land was part plough and part pasture. In addition to hunting this country, the Albany also hunted over a wide area of England, by invitation, to show sport to members of the B.H.C. in other regions.

Albany with Joint Master and Huntsman, Mr Keith Deacon, 2003.

In 1975 Mr Arthur Tucker of Spondon, Derbyshire was appointed as another Joint Master and became the Huntsman. He had whipped in to the BHC pack from the mid 1960s. In 1976 Mr P. Baker shared the hunting with Mr Tucker. In 1978 Miss M. Goodall of Oxford was elected as Chairman. In 1982 John Evans had to retire due to ill health, as did Tim Thomas. John was appointed as President of the BHC in 1983. John moved from Arkley. As a consequence, in 1981, the hounds were moved to the Westerby kennels. Arthur Tucker was joined as Joint Master by L.S. Hipkins (Hippy) of Lubenham, Market Harborough, Leicestershire. Hippy had been Field Master for many years. The hunting was taken on by Messrs J. Henshaw and C. Buckland from 1982 to 1984.

On the death of Hippy in 1986, his wife, Stella, took over the Joint Mastership. Arthur Tucker retired in 1988 and was succeeded as Joint Master by Mr Peter Baker of Morton, Derbyshire, who had hunted hounds for many years. He resigned as Huntsman in 1992 and was succeeded by Neil Kilgour. In 1992, David Money of Great Dunmow, Essex, joined Stella Hipkins as Joint Master. David's wife, Sally, became the Secretary of the Supporters Club. In the same year, Anthony Ringe of Brentwood, Essex became a third Joint Master. He and Don Peacock took on the hunting. Don had been Joint Master of the Oaston. At this time, concern was being expressed about the weight of currently bred Bassets Hounds deterring them from hunting.

In 1994 to save money and travel, hounds were transferred to kennels built by members on land owned by two members, Ron and Marion Green, at Dudden Hoe, Essex who were breeders of Basset Hounds under the prefix of Windrush. At the same time, Stella Hipkins retired as Senior Joint Master and was elected as President of the BHC, a post which she held to her death in 1998. Mrs S.F. Hughes of Rugby, Warwickshire was elected as Hunt President. In 1995 Keith Deacon was appointed as a Joint Master and, in the following year, Mr G Edwards of Ashstead, Surrey became Chairman.

In 1997 hounds returned to the Westerby kennels at livery. Mark Guy took on the post of Huntsman as he lived nearer the Westerby Kennels. Mr Michael J. Errey of Hailsham, East Sussex was elected as President in 1999 and Mrs Sally Money took on the post of Hon. Secretary, as well as continuing as Hon. Secretary of the Supporters Club. By 2000 the then Chairman of the Hunt, Peter Guy, the father of Mark and Huntsman with Keith Deacon, pointed out that, on average, only one pet Basset Hound was now hunting with the pack. The cap was now £5.

By 2001 the Albany only had seven couple of hounds in kennels as they were finding it increasingly difficult to find pure bred Basset Hounds able to hunt. To have sufficient hounds for hunting, the Albany borrowed some hounds from the Westerby. Mr G. Edwards of Ashtead, Surrey became Chairman. Use of non-KC registered Basset Hounds was controversial and resulted in the BHC withdrawing its support of the Albany in 2003. The Hunt was reformed as a separate and independent organisation and the hounds in kennels became the property of the new Committee. Keith and David retired as Joint Masters. Jeremy Ward of Preston, Hertfordshire, was elected as Master and Huntsman, having been whipping in for some years. The shortage of hounds able to hunt had to be rectified and Fourshires bloodlines were used. In 2004 three-and-a-half couple of hounds were drafted from the Huckworthy. The country was extended for the 2004/5 season by loan of the West Lodge country.

Bradley Vale (1974–1981)
Ryeford Chase Griffon Vendeen (1981–present)

Before taking the name Bradley Vale, the Hunt was formed and hunted in 1974 by Mr Nick P. Valentine as a private pack when he was in Herefordshire. The hounds were originally Petit Basset Griffon Vendéen which were outcrossed with English bassets. In 1977 Nick moved with the pack to Mid-Wales. They were then hunted in Kent during the 1978–1979 season and then in Ireland for the 1979–1980 season. In 1981 Nick

Bradley Vale with Master and Huntsman Nick Valentine at Althorp Park, Northamptonshire, 1993.

moved to Bradley Farm, Mitcheldene, Gloucestershire. The hounds were kennelled at Mutloes, Mitcheldene, Gloucestershire. The pack adopted the name Bradley Vale. There were seventeen couple of rough coated, 15in bassets in 1981, owned by Nick. They met on Wednesday and bye days at his convenience. There was no subscription as it was a private pack. The uniform adopted was a green coat and cap. In 1981 Ros Acland of Clavering, Essex, who also whipped in, was appointed as Hon. Secretary. The pack had increased to twenty couple by addition of some Basset Fauve de Bretagne.

In 1995 Mr Valentine moved to Ryeford, Ross-on-Wye, Herefordshire and the hunt was renamed. The pack had increased to thirty couple of rough coated 15in Basset Griffon Vendéen and Basset Fauve de Bretagne, together with 4 couple of working, imported wire-haired Dachshunds which act in the capacity of terriers, the hunt now also hunt fox as well as rabbit and hare. Subscriptions were taken, although the pack remained a private one. Nick Valentine also took on the post of Hon. Secretary in that year. By 1999 the number of Dachshunds had been increased to eight couple. By 2000 the pack was hunting on Wednesdays, Saturdays and Sundays and other days at the Master's convenience. By 2002 this had increased to all days of the week.

The country hunted from 1981 was northern Gloucestershire between Gloucester, Tewkesbury, Newent and Ross-on-Wye and extends into the Forest of Dene. It varied from open arable farmland, pasture and orchards, to much woodland in the Dene area. For these reasons, both rabbit and hare were hunted, according to the suitability of the terrain. By 2000, several Invitation Meets were taking place in Shropshire, Northamptonshire, Norfolk and other Counties.

* *East Lincolnshire Harehounds (1975-to present)*

The Hunt was formed in 1975 when Mr Rory Dicker of the Test Valley moved to Ireland taking his beagles with him. He donated the bassets to a Committee, who also

East Lincolnshire with Joint Master and Huntsman, Mr Mark Guy, 2004

received drafts from the Westerby and, in 1977, from the Huckworthy. Mr A. David Hindle of Louth, Lincolnshire, was appointed as Master. David is currently the Chairman of the MBHA. Mrs Hindle and Mr A.D. Lonsdale of Tattershull, Lincolnshire acted as Hon. Secretaries. In 1976 the Committee appointed Mr D. Farrant of Boston, Lincolnshire as Master and Huntsman. Mr Peter (Paddy) Castles of Coningsby, Lincolnshire was appointed as Huntsman. Meets were on alternate Wednesdays and Saturdays. Subscriptions were five guineas with a 30p. cap. The country is the marshes between Mablethorpe in the north and Wainfleet in the south. The sea to the east and The Wolds to the west. The hounds hunt within the boundaries of the South Wold Foxhounds. The Per Ardua (R.A.F.) Beagles adjoin to the west. The Test Valley uniform was retained of a black coat with a fawn collar and breeches with an evening dress of a black coat with a fawn collar and yellow silk facings. A green cap was worn.

The policy of the Committee was to breed along the lines of the Westerby and this has been pursued with occasional inputs of blood lines and drafts from the Fourshires, Huckworthy and Leadon Vale. In 1977 the kennels were moved to Hurn Bridge, Dogdyke, Coningsby, Lincolnshire. In 1979 Major O.R. Giles, TD of Boston, Lincolnshire and Mrs O. Weston of Coningsly, Lincolnshire took on the Joint Mastership and Mr L.G. Atkins of Boston, Lincolnshire became Hon. Secretary with Mrs M.R. Giles of Boston, Lincolnshire as Meets Secretary.

Paddy Castles was appointed as Joint Master in 1980. In the same year, the kennels for the seventeen couple of English bassets were moved to Oakdene, Welton le Marsh, Spilsby, Lincolnshire. Subscriptions were £15 with a £1 cap. In 1981 Major J.R. Darbyshire of West Burkwith, Lincolnshire took over the Joint Mastership. The subscription was increased to £20. Major Darbyshire was succeeded in 1982 by Mr G.A. Crust of Spilsby, Lincolnshire. The huntsman was then A.D. Lonsdale. He was succeeded in 1983 by Mr S. Brocklehurst, who had been whipping-in. Mr C. Cooper of Louth, Lincolnshire took on the Joint Mastership in 1984. By 1986 the subscriptions had had to be increased to £30, £25 for over 60s , £10 for under 18s, £1 subscribers cap and £2 cap for non-subscribers. Priscilla Ruff of Alford, Lincolnshire took on the post of Hon. Secretary in 1990. In the following year Mr D.J. Douglas of Spilsby, Lincolnshire, who had provided the kennels for the Hunt for over ten years, became Joint Master. At the same time, Richard Hill took on the hunting. The subscription was raised to £40, £70 for a family, £20 for an associate and £10 for a student with caps of £2 and £3 for visitors.

The Joint Mastership changed again in 1992 with the appointment of Mr J.D. Ramsden of Grimsby, Lincolnshire; and of Mr Steve D. Little of Martin, Lincolnshire. The Secretary's post passed to Mrs M. Manderson of Spilsby, Lincolnshire. Mrs Manderson was succeeded in 1993 by Mr E.A. Strange of Lincoln, who also took on the hunting of hounds. Mr Strange later gave up his posts to Miss S.M. Audis of Martin, Lincolnshire (Hon. Secretary) and Gavin Perry (Huntsman). The subscriptions rose to £50 and £90 for a family with a cap of £3. Mr T.R. Pearson of Metheringham, Lincolnshire became Joint Master in 1996 when Mr Ramsden moved and became Hon. Secretary.

At the end of the 1997/8 season, the hounds were moved to livery with the Holderness Hunt under their Kennel Huntsman, Robert Howarth. Mr J.D. Ramsden, now of Louth, Lincolnshire, became Joint Master again, having relinquished his Mastership in 1996. Stuart Nelson took on the post of amateur Huntsman in the same year. A Chairman, Mrs J.S. Nelson of Aldbrough, Lincolnshire, was appointed and Mrs

East Lincolnshire, 1993.

J. Elkington of Sleaford, Lincolnshire took on the post of Hon. Secretary. To cover the increased costs from livery, the subscriptions were changed to £60 and £100 for a family. Steve Little became Chairman in 1999 and Mark Guy became amateur Huntsman, having moved to Nottingham to lecture at the University and relinquishing his post with the Albany. By 2000 there were twenty couple of bassets in kennel.

Mr Ramsden retired as Joint Master in 2001 and two new Joint Masters were appointed: Mark Guy and Mr Matthew Lee of Lincoln. Matthew's grand parents had been followers of the De Burgh and his father associated with the Albany. At the same time, Simon King became Chairman and Mrs Sharon Brown of Market Rasen, Lincolnshire took on the post of Hon. Secretary. Matthew had to relinquish his Mastership in 2004 to concentrate on his professional studies as an architect. In the same year three-and-a-half couple of hounds were received as drafts form the Huckworthy.

* *Crealy (1977–1989)*

The Crealy were formed in 1977 by Mr C.J.H. Takle of Countess Wear, Devon as Master and Huntsman with his wife as Hon. Secretary. They owned nine-and-a-half couple of KC registered Basset Hounds from a number of private breeders as well as their own breeding and kennelled at Owleshayes, Aylesbeare, near Exeter under the Kennel Huntsman Mr B.J. Miller. Meets were on Saturday and occasional bye days. There was no subscription, but a cap of 50p. The uniform was a green coat. The country lay in the East Devon Foxhounds country and formed a rectangle between Budleigh Salterton-Limpstone-Westhill and Honiton. It was mainly pasture with some arable and was on loan from Stoke Hill Beagles. Between 1979 and 1982 they introduced litters from the Huckworthy and the Westerby. The pack had grown to 17 couple by 1980. In 1983 Mrs Shirley Kesler of Chumleigh, Devon took over the post of Hon. Secretary and the kennels moved to her farm. Mr A.J. Kesler took over as Huntsman. Hunting was increased to two days a week, Tuesday and Saturday. By then subscriptions had been introduced of £15 for an adult, £20 for a family and £10 for farmers, with a cap of £1. However, the Hunt was disbanded in 1989.

* *Rallye Beauvautrait (1996–2004)*

In 1994 Mr A Spillane came to England from Beauvautrait, La Tournelle du Parc, Charente, France and lived at Alburgh, Norfolk. In that year and the next, he imported from France four couple of pure bred Basset Bleu de Gascogne of four bloodlines. He registered a country in Norfolk and formed the Hunt in 1996. Mr J.P.N. Lowe of Benagle, Suffolk was Joint Master, Mrs Spillane was Hon. Secretary and Messrs. Lowe and N. Green were Huntsmen. The uniform was a black coat with a sky blue collar, cuffs and waistcoat, and black stockings. The hounds were kennelled at Albrugh, Norfolk and were the property of Mr and Mrs Spillane. It was a private pack hunting on Saturdays and occasional bye-days. Mr Spillane had the intention of the pack being kept as pure bred and of importing further bloodlines. The country extended over an area of twenty-one miles by nine miles, centred on Filby. It was a mixture of arable, marshland grazing and grass. From the foundation stock, Mr Spillane bred litters in 1996 and 1998, registering the whelps with the Kennel Club, as well as hunting them.

In 1998 Mr Stuart Brookes of Repps with Bastwick, Norfolk succeeded Mr Lowe as Joint Master and Mr Spillane returned to France. The ownership of the hounds passed to Stuart. In 1999 new arrangements had to be made for kennelling hounds and Stuart arranged to loan the four-and-a-half couple to the Black Mountain in Wales with a stipulation that any progeny from the bitches would remain his property. The intention was to retain the country until such time that hounds could be accommodated. Progeny continued to be registered with the Kennel Club. From 2000 the hounds were being hunted in Wales with the Black Mountain. By 2004 the MBHA formally recognised that the Hunt had been disbanded. The hounds were put on permanent loan to Mr Williams. The Hunt formally ceased in 2004.

* *Black Mountain (1998–present)*

The private pack was formed by Mr John Williams of Ystradgynlais, Glamorgan in 1998 with hounds from the Ryeford Chase, kennelled at Ystradgynlais. The country and the Hunt were registered at the end of the 1998–9 season. John acted as Master and Hon. Secretary with Alan Ashley as Huntsman. There were four-and-a-half couple of Basset Griffon Vendéen. Three-and-a-half couple of Basset Bleu de Gascogne were added in 1999 on loan from the Rallye Beauvautrait. The country was in Carmarthenshire and runs from the Black Mountains to Carmarthen, south to the River Taff, by kind permission of the Llandero Farmers and Carmarthenshire Foxhounds. The country had strong running hares and has spectacular scenery.

In 2000 Ralph Langdon took on the hunting, by which time there were five couple of Basset Griffon Vendéen, together with the three-and-a-half couple of Basset Bleu de Gascogne. The remaining bassets of the Rallye Beauvautrait were received in 2003 and the loan became permanent with the cessation of the Rallye Beauvautrait in 2004. The breeding policy then moved away from rough coated Basset Griffon Vendéen to a cross between these and the smooth coated Basset Bleu de Gascogne to reduce fighting in kennels and to get a more handy pack.

Mr Lett's (1998–present)

Martin Letts of Woolner, Northumberland was Master of the College Valley Foxhounds. In 1998 he formed a private pack of bassets.

Morfe Valley (2001–present)

David Vaughan of Bridgnorth, Shropshire started hunting at the age of eight, his family being in horses. He relates how his father was taken to Court for allowing him to miss school for mid-week hunts. His ambition was always to have his own pack and, in 1991, he obtained a number of bassets which had been retired from the Leadon Vale and started to hunt rabbit. He named his hunt the Morfe Valley after his favourite pub, The Red Lion of Morfe. This stands near the Morfe wood, a remnant of a Tudor hunting forest. The Bradley Vale later drafted some griffon and fauve bassets and David tried out crosses with these and with terriers, not successful, and English bassets. In 1991 he changed to hunting hare. Finding his rough coated hounds prone to hunting the heel line, he has recently added two-and-a-half couples of beagles. He has twelve to fourteen couples of hounds, kennelled at a relative's farm, looked after by David and two of his employees. The pack hunts by invitation mainly in Shropshire and Worcestershire and largely on land farmed by his relatives and friends. Following is by invitation only with donations optional. The Hunt uniform is blue breeches with burgundy socks and waistcoat, a hacking jacket and plain flat cap.

List of Masters by Hunt

HUNT	MASTER	From (1st)	To
Albany	E J Evans	1972	1982
Albany	T D Thomas	1972	1982
Albany	A Tucker	1975	1982
Albany	L S Hipkins	1981	1986
Albany	Mrs S F I Hipkins	1986	1994
Albany	P E Baker	1987	1991
Albany	A M Ringe	1992	1994
Albany	D Money	1992	2003
Albany	K Deacon	1995	2003
Albany	J Ward	2003	2004
BHC (original)	Mr Etherwood	1885	1885
BHC (present)	A J McDonald	1955	1972
BHC of Ireland	D Kennedy	1966	1976
BHC of Ireland	D O'Connor	1977	1980
BHC of Ireland	D P Dowdall	1980	1989
Black Mountain	J Williams	1998	2004
Bradley Vale	N P Valentine	1974	1981
Brancaster	Miss E Adams	1923	1933
Brighton	Maj. Croker	1887	1887
Buckland	Miss N G Holford	1908	1912
Burgonet	Mrs W Burgess	1959	1975
Captain R Law's	R Law	1935	1939
Castle Milk	A R J B-Jardine, MC	1938	1962
Chiddingstone	Mr E H M Denny	1897	1903
Col. Reynardson's	Col. Reynardson	1900	1901
Cookridge	J A Paul	1893	1897
Craigcleuch	S D B-Jones-Stamp	1959	1964
Craigcleuch	D Kirk	1964	1966
Craigcleuch	A Morris	1966	1968
Crealy	C J H Takle	1977	1986
Crealy	M J Bridgeman	1986	1988
Crealy	C J H Takle	1988	1988
Crowcombe	T F Trollope-Bellew	1948	1964
Crowcombe	Mrs T F T-Bellew	1951	1964
Dalby Hall	Miss L B-Hartopp	1906	1931
Dalby Hall	Hon. E Nicholson	1916	1919
Dalby Hall	R F P Monckton	1926	1926

HUNT	MASTER	From (1st)	To
Dalby Hall	Maj. Hodgkin	1927	1927
Dale Park	C Fletcher	1888	1893
Delapré	Mr C Cooper	1894	1904
Dallam Tower	Sir M B-Wilson	1898	1914
Danebury	M Cannon	1885	1890
Danebury	T Cannon	1885	1890
De Burgh	R E Way	1960	1971
De Burgh	J S Humphrey	1971	1997
De Burgh	P E Bassett	1992	1997
De Burgh	C J Townrow	1995	1997
De Burgh	Mrs E Philp	1997	present
De Burgh	P Thomas	2000	present
Delapré	C Cooper	1894	1904
Delapré	R Cooper	1894	1904
East Lincolnshire	A D Hindle	1975	1978
East Lincolnshire	D Farrant	1976	1977
East Lincolnshire	O R Giles	1979	1980
East Lincolnshire	Mrs O Weston	1979	1994
East Lincolnshire	P Castles	1980	1981
East Lincolnshire	J R Darbyshire	1981	1982
East Lincolnshire	L G Atkins	1982	1984
East Lincolnshire	G A Crust	1982	1987
East Lincolnshire	C Cooper	1984	1989
East Lincolnshire	D J Douglas	1991	1992
East Lincolnshire	J D Ramsden	1992	1996
East Lincolnshire	S D Little	1992	present
East Lincolnshire	E A Strange	1993	1994
East Lincolnshire	T R Pearson	1996	2000
East Lincolnshire	J D Ramsden	1998	2001
East Lincolnshire	M Lee	2001	2003
East Lincolnshire	M Guy	2001	present
East Lincolnshire	R Furness	2004	2004
East Suffolk	C G L Marriott	1961	1967
East Suffolk	Mrs C G L Marriott	1961	1967
Easthampstead	A C C Kenyon Fuller	1881	1893
Eastington Park	C de Lisle Bush	1928	1940
Fairforth	F H Temperley	1909	1910
Fairforth	H I Jones	1910	1916
Fairforth	A E Leonard	1913	1916
Fourshires	C D Meredith	1963	1976
Fourshires	M McDermott	1964	1966
Fourshires	Mrs M S Argles	1966	1969
Fourshires	D A Lloyd	1970	1975
Fourshires	J H Lloyd	1975	1985
Fourshires	R M Gardener	1979	1984
Fourshires	R D Schuster	1984	1990
Fourshires	C D Meredith	1986	1990
Fourshires	C Cottrell-Dormer	1991	present
Fourshires	Lady Higgs	1991	present
Fourshires	J Cordingley	1995	present
Fourshires	A Coupe	1998	2000
Greywell Hill	Hon. D Carleton	1902	1914
Greywell Hill	Marq. of Devonshire	1904	1906
Grims	Miss M M Keevil	1951	1964

HUNT	MASTER	From (1st)	To
Herefordshire	R Hudson	1958	1966
Highworth	C E Hanbury	1896	1900
Huckworthy	C. H Parlby	1967	1971
Huckworthy	Mrs A Parlby	1967	2004
Huckworthy	C P T Rebbeck	1971	1979
Huckworthy	P C Mott	1973	2004
Huckworthy	D Schreiber	1979	1981
Huckworthy	A T MacCaw	1981	1985
Huckworthy	T MacCaw	1981	1985
Huckworthy	J Parkes, OBE	2001	2002
Hyndfar	D Evans	1982	1984
Hyndfar	D G Rees, MD, ChB	1982	1984
Iwerne Minster	Miss D Isamy	1913	1917
Jocelyn Lucas's	J Lucas	1913	1914
Kilspindie	H ap Evans, MC	1956	1960
Kilspindie	H Drummond	1956	1969
Kilspindie	A Drummond	1959	1969
Knowlton	Miss G Peto	1900	1900
Lancers, 17th	Maj. Fitzhugh	1939	1940
Leadon Vale	D Mann	1967	1996
Leadon Vale	E C Mansell	1968	1969
Leadon Vale	T G Mayo	1971	1972
Leadon Vale	B E Wilson	1971	1973
Leadon Vale	R Taylor	1974	1974
Leadon Vale	M W Tytherleigh	1974	1975
Leadon Vale	R S Smith	1974	1980
Leadon Vale	D Taylor	1976	1978
Leadon Vale	C J Welch	1978	1979
Leadon Vale	G I Tustin	1979	1980
Leadon Vale	D K Oliver	1980	1996
Leadon Vale	D J Philpotts	1986	1993
Leadon Vale	C H Grinnall	1994	1996
Leadon Vale	A Greenwood	1994	2000
Leadon Vale	B Read	1996	1997
Leadon Vale	Mrs M P Major	1997	2001
Leadon Vale	S Evans	1999	present
Leadon Vale	M Whitehead	2000	present
Lord Onslow's	Lord Onslow	1872	1884
Lord Tredegar's	Lord Tredegar	1914	1919
Lord Tredegar's	Lord Tredegar	1928	1933
Major Kemmis's	Maj. Kemmis	1903	1904
Major Wilkie's	Maj. Wilkie	1928	1929
Melancthon	Mrs W M Aspin	1968	2002
Mid-Down	D G Rees, MB, ChB	1968	1972
Miss Barlow's	Miss F Barlow	1937	1938
Morfe Valley	D. Vaughan	2001	present
Mr Baylay's	Mr Baylay	1903	1904
Mr Duff-A-Smith's	B W D-A-Smith	1896	1897
Mr M. J Letts's	M J Letts	1998	present
Mr M B Kennedy's	M B Kennedy	1881	1887
Mr Mellor's	Mr Mellor	1938	1939
Mr V Fleming's	V Fleming	1911	1915
Mr Vincent Eyre's	V Eyre	1900	1901
Mr Woodhouse's	A N L Woodhouse	1884	1890

HUNT	MASTER	From (1st)	To
Mursley	Viscount Malden	1908	1910
Myola Park	Lt. Col. R Spencer	1898	1899
N. Warwickshire	R W Wright	1955	1965
N'tonshire Yeoman.	Mr Lowinger	1940	1947
North Lancashire	Y B Olive	1907	1911
North Lancashire	T B Forwood	1907	1911
Oaston	C H Frisby	1963	1964
Oaston	E Ball	1964	1966
Oaston	R H A Milligan	1964	1968
Oaston	J E Walker	1965	1966
Oaston	C M Faulkes	1968	1971
Oaston	T Twigger	1968	1971
Oaston	D A Peacock	1971	1975
Oaston	R H C Pickering	1971	1975
Oaston	D R Hands	1972	1975
Oaston	Mrs M Pickering	1972	1975
Petre Uchaf	D G Rees, MD, ChB	1973	1982
Petre Uchaf	D Evans	1975	1982
Polebrooke	Maj. V Ferguson	1893	1896
Rallye Beauvautrait	A Spillane	1996	1998
Rallye Beauvautrait	J P N Lowe	1996	1998
Rallye Beauvautrait	S Brooks	1998	2004
Reepham	H C Swan	1902	1903
Reepham	N C Swan	1902	1903
Ringwould	W Marsh	1961	1964
Riversdale	Mr J L Bulcock	1886	1890
Riversfield	A F Towgood	1903	1913
Ross-shire	D G Rees, MD, ChB	1972	1973
Royal Tank Corps	L B Ball	1919	1920
Royal Tank Corps	G McClintock	1920	1923
Royal Tank Corps	F R Hope, CBE, DSO	1923	1925
Royal Tank Corps	D F M Tudor	1925	1926
Ryeford Chase	N. Valentine	1981	present
Sandringham	King Edward VII	1884	1910
Sandringham	Queen Alexandra	1884	1922
Scalford Hall	G Colman, OBE, TD	1940	1954
Sir Jocelyn Lucas's	Sir J Lucas, MC, MP	1955	1958
Sitka	D. Teichman, DSO, MC	1902	?
Sitka	Mr MacIntyre	?	1908
Slane	Marq. of Conygham	1903	1910
South Wales	N Harby	1966	1969
South Wales	N P Thomas, MBE,	1966	1973
South Wales	G Vaughan	1966	1978
South Wales	Lady Treherne, OBE	1966	1985
South Wales	T Keen	1970	1977
South Wales	I E Symonds, CBE	1973	1989
South Wales	C E Harrison, JP	1978	1985
South Wales	W R Bishop	1983	1987
South Wales	Mrs C E Harrison	1985	1996
South Wales	J A Roberts	1989	1997
South Wales	S A Wenham	1993	1996
South Wales	Mrs J Rees	1996	1998
Stainrigg	J Little	1902	1912
Stevenstone	F T Sumner	1968	1972

HUNT	MASTER	From (1st)	To
Stoodleigh	E H Dunning	1900	1901
Street Ashton	Q O Gold	1902	1902
Test Valley	R Dicker	1969	1975
Walhampton (a)	C Heseltine	1890	1903
Walhampton (a)	G Heseltine	1890	1903
Walhampton (b)	G Heseltine	1890	1914
Walhampton (c)	Hon. E Nicholson	1916	1918
Walhampton (d)	C H Carter	1918	1919
Walhampton (d)	C Aldin	1918	1919
Walhampton (e)	G Heseltine	1920	1932
Walhampton (e)	Mrs G Heseltine	1932	1933
Walhampton (e)	E F S Morrison, MC	1932	1933
Waltham	Hon. Mrs E Greenall	1933	1937
West Lodge	L R Woolner	1950	1966
West Lodge	E Shelley	1951	1953
West Lodge	B H Sheppard	1953	1957
West Lodge	R Brooks-Ward	1958	1971
West Lodge	J Eden	1961	1969
West Lodge	E D Dawson	1961	1971
West Lodge	J P-Williams, OBE	1971	1985
West Lodge	H W C Denby-Wood	1976	1980
West Lodge	A King-Cline	1977	1986
West Lodge	N J F Curtiss	1983	1997
West Lodge	J E Grande	1987	1993
West Lodge	W Burton	1993	1997
West Lodge	Mrs G Willis	1993	2002
West Lodge	H W C Denby-Wood	1997	present
West Lodge	M Willis	2002	present
Westerby	E F S Morrison, MC	1933	1951
Westerby	G A C Breitmeyer	1937	1939
Westerby	K Gimson	1947	1951
Westerby	R P Swain	1947	1951
Westerby	C A Weston	1951	1959
Westerby	J C E Bevin	1951	1981
Westerby	J J L Underwood	1963	1963
Westerby	D B Bragg	1978	1987
Westerby	J W E Bevin, BVM	1983	1994
Westerby	A S Jacks	1992	1994
Westerby	D M Leather	1992	present
Westerby	M Welton	1995	1997
Westerby	R E Bowers	1995	1997
Westerby	Mrs E A Burton	1999	present
Wheatley Park	Sir William Cooke	1894	1899
Wick & District	J H Hawes	1924	1928
Wick & District	E E Pratt	1924	1931
Wick & District	C Wade	1924	1931
Wick & District	J S Williams	1931	1936
Wick & District	J V Phipps	1931	1936
Wintershill	J S Moss	1889	1898
Wolvercote	?	1895	1896
Wrest Pack	J G Murray	1924	1925
Wroxton	Lord North	1907	1933

Chapter Seven

Significant Breeders and Importers

THE histories of hunts recounted in Chapter 6 does not convey the full picture of those responsible for the development of the basset in England for hunting.

The first thirty years of the modern basset in England was fed by a stream of imports from European breeders, predominantly French. This began to diminish around the close of the nineteenth century as the standards of bassets in France declined. It virtually ceased in 1901 with the introduction of the Quarantine Laws. Since then only a relatively few have been imported.

The almost complete separation of hunting from showing bassets in England is relatively new. Until the early twentieth century, both contributed to common development of the basset. Even the breakaway of hunts from the Kennel Club in 1911 with the formation of the MBHA did not entirely separate the two interests in the breed. The Walhampton and other hunts continued to enter shows and non-hunting breeders continued to supply stock to hunts. Both World Wars resulted in a severe diminution of numbers of hounds and the subsequent re-building was due to the co-operation of hunts and show kennels. Up to this day, hunts have introduced a limited amount of show stock into their gene pools.

Searches of the KC Stud Books are limited by two factors. In their first four volumes (1874–1877) there are no specific mentions of bassets. In the next five volumes (1878–1882) some entries under the category 'Foreign Dogs' are referred to as 'bassets'. Only from 1883 is there a category of 'Basset Hounds'.

This chapter gives a little background to some of these breeders and importers who have contributed so much to the development of the hunting basset. The selection of individuals for inclusion here is, of necessity, very subjective. There are many others.

In line with the previous chapter on the Hunts, the selected breeders and importers are arranged in chronological order by reference to when their influence on bassets began. An alphabetical list with the page reference in this chapter follows.

Le Comte le Couteulx de Canteleu (c. 1865)

The Comte was a son of an Officer in the army of Napoleon I and a Cavalry Officer himself. He left the Army in 1852. He was passionately interested in hounds and made many experiments to recreate some of the old French breeds.He started a Hunt in Saint-Martin on wolf, using Griffon Vendéen Nivernais hounds. One cross was a she wolf with a Griffon Vendéen doghound. He then crossed back the progeny to these hounds for three further generations until all visual resemblance to a wolf had disappeared. He had to cease this in 1862 following the death of his father. In 1870 he sold several couple of these wolf outcrosses and some Griffon de Bresse to Mr S. Waldron Hill, the Master of the East Lothian Otterhounds. It is not clear what became of these, although it is reported that some were sold to America. There is a letter in *Hounds* (Vol. 14, No. 4, 1998, Pp. 36–37) detailing this experiment.

Later the Comte sent his remaining Griffon Nivernais to Mr Richard Carnaby Forster

Bassets of the Comte de Couteulx at the Jardin d'Acclimatation, Paris, 1888.

in England. Mr Forster then gave them to his step-daughter, Lady Mary Hamilton. In 1906 these hounds were sold to various Otter Hound packs. At the same time, the Comte acquired four Saint Hubert Hounds (Bloodhounds) from Scotland.

The Comte was well aware of bassets by 1858 as he describes them in his publication *La Vénerie française*:

> Long body, short legs, large back, long leathers, lovely head, lovely voice, the Basset is full of good qualities. It always has a loathing for any beast, but rabbit and hare are particularly favoured quarry; however Bassets are a perfect pure breed for roe deer, wolf and boar.
>
> Usually white with black or fawn markings, often their hair is all black and thick with reddish touches under the eyes, over the chest and at the base of the legs. Many are griffons and amongst these, many are white with large patches of coffee colour.
>
> The other varieties of Basset are primarily distinguished by very pronounced arching of the front legs; their colour is the same as that of the straight legged bassets; only I know that the griffons are very rare.
>
> The Bassets are naturally very much slower than the other hounds.
>
> Their perfidious slowness, which makes hunting hare a mistake and makes them scamper along in front of them in amazement, taking all day to catch one from an infinite number of hares and roe-deer.
>
> The Basset is easy to breed and will hunt from eight or nine months old.

The Comte may have started a kennel of bassets at Etrepagny sometime before 1866 as those sent to Lord Galway in that year were said to have been bred by the Comte. The origins of these bassets are unclear. The Comte referred to them as Basset d'Artois and, in 1890, attributed their origin to the Basset d'Artois and la Flandre. Some authorities maintain that these had never died out and that the Comte preserved them. But the Comte, again in 1890, stated that they had been lost since 1860 as he had searched 'the world' for them without success and had had to entirely rebreed them with Monsieur Louis Lane. He then described his bassets as follows:

> The Basset is very tough and perfect for hunting to the gun. Very brave, one can hunt all quarry. Generally having a lovely cry, they supply it abundantly and four Bassets make as much music as a pack. Because they always go at a careful pace with moderation, because of their structure, the quarry is not scared by the pursuit and, gambling along ahead of them, it can easily be shot: however our Bassets are sufficiently active and can account for a hare.

They are thought to have been smooth haired, usually tricolour, 28 to 30 cm, and straight or semi-crooked with deeply sunken dark eyes and with a prominent haw. The heads were long, domed and narrow.Comte Élie de Vezin in his1882 book says that the Comte described his bassets thus:

> The hound, to be well-made and beautiful, should have the head well-made and longer than it is broad; the forehead wide; the eye large and bright; the nostrils well-opened and moist rather than dry; the ear low, narrow, hanging down and curled inwards and longer than the nose by only two inches. The body of a size and length proportionate to the limbs so that without being too long it may be more slender than stocky; the shoulders neither too wide nor too narrow; the back broad, high and arched; the haunches high and wide; the stern broad near the back but terminating like that of a rat and loosely curved in a half-circle; the thighs well tucked up and well muscled; the leg vigorous, the foot lean and the nails thick and short.

The Comte was an authority on the history, origins and genealogy of hounds, about which he wrote several books between 1858 and 1890. He is generally acknowledged to have started the late nineteenth century basset. A number of his hounds were kept for breeding at Le Chenil du Jardin d'Acclimatation in Paris. This had been founded in 1870 as a national centre for animal breeding. It was from the Comte that Lord Onslow imported some of the early bassets in1874. Other hounds, either bred by the Comte or sired by his hounds in the Jardin, were later imported into England.

His influence in the establishment and development of smooth coated bassets in England can not be over emphasised. The most reliable Stud Book of the early years of bassets in England was printed as Supplements in *The Kennel Review* of 1883 and 1884 and covered hounds whelped between 1870 and 1883. Of the sixty-four hounds listed with known pedigrees, twenty-eight had one or both parents bred by the Comte and fifty-one had one or more grand parents bred by him (thirteen with one or two, twenty-eight with three or four). The Kennel Club Stud Books record ten hounds bred by the Comte: vis:

7849	Finette. Whelped 1875. Owned by the Earl of Onslow.
7850	Fino. Whelped 1875. Owned by the Earl of Onslow. Liver, white and tan.
7857	Nestor. Whelped 1876. Owned by the Earl of Onslow. Liver, white and tan.
11060	Fino de Paris. Owned by G.R. Krehl.Tricolour.
11070	Pallas. Owned by G.R. Krehl. Black, white and tan.
12138	Guinevere (or Gibelotte). Whelped 1878. Owned by G.R. Krehl. Bicolour.
15703	Theo. Owned by G.R. Krehl.
16949	Gareth. Owned by Harry Ivor Jones.
18331	St Martin. Whelped 1884. Owned by G.R. Krehl. Tricolour, black back.
21681	Le Fanfaron. Whelped 1885. Owned by F.P. Ellis. Tricolour.

Lord Galway (1866)

Lord Galway of Serlby in Nottinghamshire visited his friend, the Comte de Tournon, in France in 1866. Here he saw bassets hunting and expressed his admiration of them. It is probable that the hunting was to a gun, rather than as a pack. As a result, the Comte sent a pair of bassets to Lord Galway in the same year. These were smooth coated. Lord Galway gave them the names of Basset and Belle. He mated them and Belle whelped in 1867.

The scant evidence is that these hounds had been bred by the Comte de Couteulx in his attempts to re-create the old Normand and Artois hounds. The few photographs show them to be crooked, smooth coated, tricolour and with large heads and longish ears. They were of a substance, some way between the modern Basset Hound and the modern Basset Artésien-Normand. This is hardly surprising as both breeds have been developed from this type.

It is not known whether Lord Galway either hunted these hounds or kept them as mere curiosities. What is known is that, about 1872, Lord Galway sold the entire three and half couple to Lord Onslow.

Most of this is known because of a letter written many years later by Lord Galway to Major Godfrey Heseltine recalling the events:

> In July 1866, 1 was staying at Royat, Pay de Dome. France. where I met the Marquis de Tournon and his son the Comte de Tournon. The latter promised me a couple of Basset Hounds from his pack, which duly arrived later in the autumn at Serlby. They were a dog

> and a bitch, and I called them Basset and Belle. They were long, low hounds, shaped much like a Dachshund with crooked forelegs at the knees with much more bone and larger heads than our Beagles. They were not the dark tan colour of the Dachshund but the colour of Fox-hounds with a certain amount of white about them. They had deep, heavy bones, more like Foxhounds than Beagles. I mated these two in 1867, and had a litter of five, all of which survive. I remember I called one Bellman. I sold these three and a half couples to the late Lord Onslow in, I think, 1872, but I am not quite sure of the date.

Whilst Lord Galway was, almost certainly, not the first owner of bassets in England, this importation and litter marked the beginning of the modern basset in England. It led to the development of the Basset Hound as a distinct breed and the development of bassets for hunting in England.

Monsieur Louis Lane (1870)

Louis Lane lived at the Châteaux de Franqueville, near Rouen, France. He is believed have become involved with bassets about 1870. He said that he obtained two bitches from Monsieur Flour of Doullens, Artois. The Comte le Couteulx maintained that the Lane bassets were the same origins as his own.

Louis Lane aimed to quickly build up a basset clearly resembling the old Norman hound, but with some characteristics of the more athletic Artois hound. In comparison with the Couteulx type, the Lane type was low, heavily boned, large and wide apple-shaped heads, deep muzzles and flews, big and prominent eyes, inclined to have cheek bumps, very hairy, loaded at the shoulder, full crooked and short legs, thin ears, a slim stern, powerful, energetic and with a beautiful cry. They tended to be pale tan and white, lemon and white or badger pied, rather than the darker tricolours and bicolours of the Couteulx type. Whilst they were tenacious and found to be useful for hunting in woods with a good voice, they lacked drive and were slow. They also tended to knuckle over. Compared to the Couteulx type, they were larger, heavier and taller.

Monsieur Louis Lane's bassets exhibited in 1878.

One of the modern authorities on bassets, Maurice Leblanc, in his 1995 book describes the Lane basset as follows;

> The nose is well developed, the muzzle long, sometimes slightly hooked, it is separated from the forehead by a less pronounced angle than that of the Basset of Le Couteulx. The chops are slightly accentuated and the brow, high and narrow, showing the beauty of the breed. The eyes are usually slightly clear, the cheeks pulled up and well formed; superb leathers, long, finely attached and curling, placed below the line of the eye, never flat; the neck is long and slight, (total absence of dewlap); the chest is big and wide. The body long, massive and near to the ground, the shoulders slightly straight, the elbows pointing outwards, the back strong and large. The stern like a candle, well attached, fine hair, rear quarters with powerful muscles, the legs crooked, large feet turned outwards.
>
> Height between 30 and 32 cm at the shoulders.
>
> Tricolour coloured, yet light colours without being bright like those of the Bassets of Le Couteulx and hounds with such a coat are fairly rare. This breed has produced hounds which were white and orange.

Monsieur Leasable in an article of 1884 :

> Somewhat reluctant to draw, they need to be watched and gradually coaxed on to the line. Slightly ambitious, docile, come back well, they bring requisite values to the working of a pack.
>
> Slower and less sprightly than the Bassets of Le Couteulx, plenty of material to be worked on, they are difficult to work in gorse or brambles. They get tangled up in the Solonge heathers, they can not get out nor work in these conditions.

Whilst the Lane basset became very popular in France in the late 1870s and 1880s, they were not so well favoured in England initially as the Couteulx type was more active, lighter and more suited for hunting. The Lane breeding were sometimes referred to as the 'norman' type the Couteulx breeding as the 'artésien'. To confuse matters, both were still called 'Basset d'Artois' in Mimard & Blachon's book of 1907.

George Krehl imported the first two Lane bassets in 1882: Blanchette and Oriflamme (15702). He also imported Lane's Gavotte (18348). These may have followed Lane's showing in England of his Clochette (12147) the previous year. Over the next few years Lane continued to show in England and at least five other Lane bred bassets were imported: Bavard (16257), Chorister (16539), Ramono II (21683), Cunegonde (21692) and Champion (23786).

However, only Blanchette was used to any extent by the hunts in England and the other Lane bassets were used only sparingly by the English show breeders. Nevertheless, it was a combination of the Couteulx type and the Lane type, together with later outcrossing, which became the Basset Hound in England. In France the two types were used almost exclusively to produce the present day Basset Artésien-Normand. In this sense, Louis Lane, with Comte le Couteulx, can truly be said to have created the two main present day smooth haired bassets breeds.

Sir Everett Millais (1874)

Everett Millais was a son of the artist, Sir John Millais. He was a fairly wealthy man and was later knighted. In the 1870s he resided in South Kensington, London. His interest in dogs began early in his life and, by 1874, he owned a Dachshund, Chenda (6339). He also came to own Dachs (4483) Both had been bred by his brother, J.G. Millais of Alford, Lincolnshire, who had obtained his stock from the Royal Kennels in Hanover.

Millais's interest in Dachshunds probably was part of the craze for them triggered by Prince Edward of Saxe-Weimer presenting some to his relative, Prince Albert, following his marriage to Queen Victoria in 1840. Prince Albert kept them at Windsor and used them to drive pheasants to the guns. At that time, they were known in England as German Badger Hounds. As a result of this Royal patronage, they became very popular in England. So much so that between, 1876 and 1877, a Mr Schuller, is said to have imported 200 of them.

Many of the early owners of bassets had Dachshunds. Indeed, bassets were often asserted to be crosses between Dachshunds and Beagles. As a result, almost to the end of the nineteenth century, bassets were often judged with dachshunds and, for many years, basset classes were often judged by dachshund judges. Consequently the shift of interest of some individuals from Dachshunds to bassets was quite natural and may have accounted for the initial interest of Everett Millais, as it may have done for Lord Onslow. Also, in these early days, the close association undoubtedly influenced the thinking of breeders, including Millais, especially on the possibility of a common ancestry of bassets and Dachshunds. This would have been reinforced by the French referring to 'Basset Allemande'. Even in their book of 1907, Mimard and Blanchon refer to 'Tekel (Dachshund) or Basset Allemande'. Millais is quoted as saying:

> As in Germany anything with crooked legs is called a Dachshund. so in France for the same reason 'the anything' is called Chien Basset, for the simple reason that the people do not know better. In England it is the same; the Terrier is good enough for the whole race whether pure or mongrel.

In 1874, the year Millais imported his first basset, Model (7854) from the Jardin d'Acclimatation. Model had been bred by the Comte le Couteulx and was straight legged. Model was quite different to some of the heavily crooked bassets imported by Lord Galway and bred by Lord Onslow, as can be seen from the accompanying Table

	Fino	Model
Age	3 years	4 years
Height at the shoulder	33 cm	30.5 cm
Length from the occiput to the end of the nose	25.5 cm	23 cm
Length from the nose to the origin of the stern	84 cm	82 cm
Length of the stern	28 cm	29 cm
Breadth of the chest	61 cm	63 cm
Breadth at the stomach	58.5 cm	53 cm
Weight	18 kg	21 kg

Both Everett and his brother, J.G. Millais, had been strongly influenced in the ideas of evolution and the inheritance of observed characteristics expounded by Darwin in his books of 1859, 1868 and 1871. Later, these are all alluded to Everett Millais's lecture of 1895. This lecture described Everett's later work on crossing bassets with Bloodhounds.

It is also clear from his St Thomas' lecture that Everett Millais was influenced by the concept of telegony then being propounded by a Mr Herbert Spencer. Telegony suggested that characteristics of the members of one litter could be influenced by previous sires of the bitch as well as by the immediate sire. This concept was troubling breeders of many animals through to the opening of the second half of the twentieth century.

Millais summarised much of his work in 1884 in *The Kennel Review* (Vol. II, No. 20,

Pp. 230–232). This is reproduced in full here as the influence of Millais on the basset and his thinking have been so important in the development of the basset worldwide. It also contains advice that we would do well to follow today.

The Rise of the BASSET-HOUND
FROM 1875 TO 1884

It is just ten years, almost to a day, since I first saw a Basset, and the Basset has been to me ever since the chef-d'oeuvre of the canine world.

I forget really what led me to the Jardin d'Acclimatation that never-to-be-forgotten day ten years ago, but I have a shrewd idea that it was to see the Dachshunds kennelled there, and to compare them with my little hound, of which I was then, and am still, an admirer.

Nor shall I ever forget how pleased I was on recognising the unquestionable fact that my 'Dachs' was a better Dachshund than any caged there for exhibition. Nor, lastly, shall I forget with what intense admiration and surprise I viewed their next door neighbours – the Basset Français.

Dear little Dachs – for he is dear little Dachs still -I am afraid had even then in his youth few charms in comparison with his larger and gayer-marked French cousins.

He was yellow, whereas those he gazed upon were much bigger, with black and white bodies and rich tan heads, more beautiful than Dachs, with soft, dreamy eyes.

What could I do but wish for one, and my desire was soon gratified, for a communication with Comte Couteulx had the desired effect.

There were two dogs there so much alike, that it was with difficulty I could distinguish between them.

The one I claimed is now known to Basset-lovers in England by the name of Model. The other was Fino de Paris [11060], perhaps better known as Mr Krehl's champion, but at that date Mr Krehl had not seen a Basset.

So much for how I obtained my first Basset.

I had then no intention of showing dogs in England or elsewhere. I had bought the Dachshund because I liked the funny, crook-legged little fellow, and for the same reason I bought the Basset.

But at the end of the year 1874, when I came over to England, and I remember well Model was dreadfully sick whilst crossing the Channel, the spirit of envy seized upon me when Mr John Temperley, whose younger brother is our latest addition to the 'fancy,' informed me that he had won a prize with Dachs' sister Zampa.

I then longed to exhibit too – to have a hound that had carried off a prize; and I had not long to wait.

Wolverhampton was the show that I determined to commence at, and from this date I propose to trace the gradual rise of the Basset until the present year, and also the beautiful hounds the uses we make to mark out what the future of should or ought to be, according to the material that is at our disposal.

To do so, I intend to divide the decade which has gone by into four progressive stages, which periods follow one another as follows :-

1. From the importation of Model, and my attempts at breeding Bassets through a Beagle till -
2. Lord Onslow's importations, and what came of them, to the Wolverhampton show of 1880.
3. Mr Krehl's and Mr Lewis Clement's (Wildfowler) importations, and the breaking up of the Earl of Onslow 's and my own kennels.

4. Mr Krehl's second importation, and the formation of the Basset Club to the present date.

FIRST PERIOD

Wolverhampton show of 1875, at which prize in the Variety class, and which show in canine animals, as being the first exhibition at which a Basset was shown, an attempt was made by some Dachshund fanciers to prove that the Basset was nothing more or less than the result of a cross between the Dachshund and a Beagle, or the result of the commixture of other blood with that Dachshund.

I felt as sure then as I do now of the error of these letters in the *Fancier's Gazette* and I am just as certain now that the principal writer of them is as sure of these errors now himself.

Notwithstanding what had been written and said against my favourite, I was nowise abashed, but, if anything, urged on to show him again, and I did so at the summer show of the Kennel Club at the Crystal Palace, 1875.

The result was a triumph – aye, more, for not only was my hound awarded first prize in the Variety class but he was acknowledged as a pure bred animal, and beautiful specimen of his race, not only by people in general, but, what was of greater worth to me, by his former detractors. This success induced me to try and breed the Basset.

I was young then, little more than a boy, and it never occurred to me then as it would now, that it would be better to try and import a bitch of the breed from France, than try and breed one myself from another species.

I have, however, always had the knack of making something do, if the right thing is not at hand, and I do not think I should be wrong in saying that I succeeded.

Thus, there being no Basset bitch in England, I resorted to breeding from a beagle- principally from the similarity in the markings, and its being the only hound low enough for a Basset to cover.

I mentioned the plan to Mr Lort, and this great authority gave me a few kind words of advice as to how I should pursue my policy.

Having, therefore, procured a beagle bitch in the points I looked for, I had her covered, and the following table will show the results

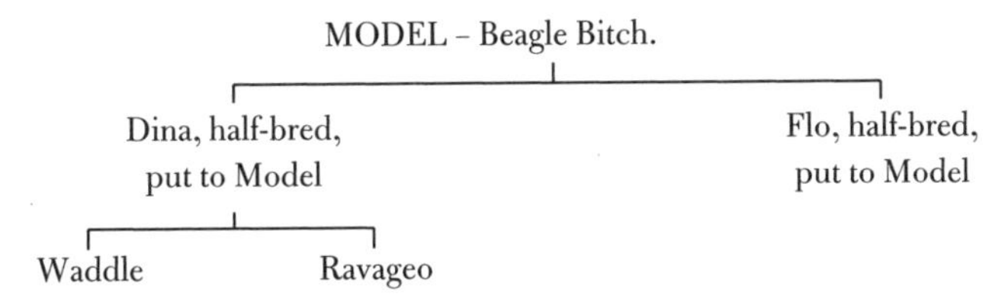

In speaking of this attempt to produce Bassets through a beagle, I do not do so with the view of others following my example. I wish it to be clearly understood that I condemn it in every way, and should it ever be resorted to, let it be only done when we have no other shift to turn to.

You will observe from the above pedigree, that Dina half-bred result of the Basset-beagle and Flo were the connection.

They were both long, low bitches – beautiful tricolours, but light in bone, and wanting in leather. Their feet and legs, perhaps one of the most essential points in the hound, were demi-torses, and, as I have frequently remarked, so powerful are the Couteulx hounds in their main characteristics, that any breed into which they are brought in blood-contact will inevitably show these peculiar trait.

When old enough, I put these two bitches to their own father (Model).

The result of this second cross produced in Dina pure, Bassets – in Flo, pups like herself.

Waddle and Ravageo have been both exhibited, the former at Brighton (1876), and the latter elsewhere. Waddle was a lemon and white dog of great bone and power, with a not over good head, and is still alive, the property of Mr Alfred Barrett, of Kingston-on-Thames, who I know would be only too happy to show him to any gentleman. Ravageo was small, no doubt from in-breeding, but he was tricolour, and was the property of Mr Perceval de Castro, of Dachshund fame.

They were both good average torse-Bassets. I was unfortunate in losing every pup except these two, and the dams went down also into that fatal scourge, distemper, followed by chorea and fits.

Here I was then, as badly off as before, but during all this time, nearly two years, I never lost an opportunity of showing in company with my friend Mr Temperley, who showed Dachshunds.

At this moment, when I was brooding over the loss of Dina and Flo, with their bitch pups, and debating with myself whether it was really worth the trouble of beginning the old beagle business over again, the Earl of Onslow came to the rescue; and here begins the second period of which I have spoken.

The Earl of Onslow commenced with a couple which he obtained from Comte Couteulx, and not satisfied with them, three more, namely, Fino, Nestor, and Finette, and at a later period, Finette he at once sent to Model, and the result that visit was the birth of Proctor and Garenne.

Proctor was a big lemon and white dog, Garenne, which his lordship allowed me to claim for the services of Model, a very beautiful tricolour bitch, but small. Through Proctor there was little in-breeding that I know of. He was put to Juno, and the result of that visit was Vesta, the dam of Franco, whom Mr Wyndham-Carter may call the father of his kennels, his Ramee dying before he obtained a litter by him, that lived long.

Out of six litters which Garenne had by her own father (Model), I only reared three puppies, namely, Isabel, Model II., and Vesta (Mr Reginald Temperley's). Garenne invariably threw her pups tail-first, and had great difficulty in getting away from them. Isabel was a lemon-and-white bitch, so was Vesta, whilst the dog, Model II., was tricolour.

I did not wish to inbreed again with Isabel to the old hound, so, with the Earl of Onslow's permission, I had her sent to Fino, but I should be wrong to say that this was not inbreeding at all, as Fino was own brother to her g.-dam, Finette. The result of this cross was the birth in August, 1879, of Ulfius and Bratias (as they are now called), Niniche, Kathleen, and Marie. The following table will give a better idea of the inbreeding than words will:-

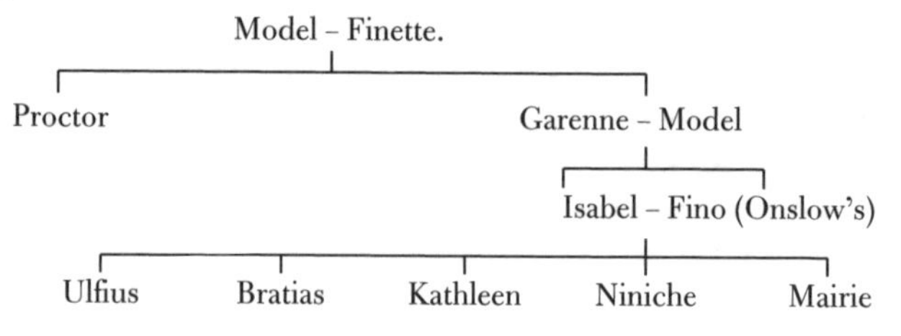

Such, then, was my kennel at the opening of 1880, when the Wolverhampton show came on.

I obtained a Basset class on the conditions that I guaranteed the entries. I did so, but there was only one competitor in addition to myself, and the exhibit was far from a Basset. However, the Wolverhampton show did one thing – it brought the hounds before the public, and I returned home with more determination than ever to form a pack.

'But man proposes,' &c., and so it was with me. I had just managed to breed a litter of pups out of Kathleen, out of her brother, Ulfius, and another by Bratias, ex Niniche when I was taken ill, and remained so until the end of the year when, under medical advice I packed up my traps and sailed for Australia.

I was, indeed, sorry to part with my pets. I sold or gave them all away with the exception of Model and Garenne, whom I did not feel able to part with. Here we enter on the third period of the decade, and it is, if not of great length, at least the most important of the four periods.

The Earl of Onslow about this period saw fit to break up or part with some of his hounds – Fino going to form the nucleus of Mr Monro's, Juno to Mr Pick, whilst my Ulfius and Bratias went to Mr Collett, Kathleen to Mr Krehl, who now entered the list of Basset-men.

The latter gentleman joined us with his marvellous Fino de Paris, Pallas, Jupiter, &c., and later on showed Pallas II, Vivien, Ygerne, Guinevere and Artemis. It is not too much to say that, if Mr Krehl had not thrown in his lot with us the Bassets in this country would have dwindled to spectres of their former selves.

About this time, also, Mr Lewis Clement introduced Ramee, a hound whose origin is as obscure as Mr Krehl's were known to be Couteulx; but one thing I am sure of namely, that if Mr Krehl had not imported his, the fillip would never have been given that made Mr Clement bring over Ramee.

From Mr Krehl's persistent and indefatigable efforts have arisen the large classes that we now see at our principal shows. It is he that has imported the fresh stock that has so helped the breed to become more general, and it is he who has imported the very best hounds the Continent could produce, and what is more I believe he has done so for the sake of the breed and not with any 'arriere-pensee' for himself or his pocket.

His Fino has got pups out of bitches whose names are common enough, but I think might well be named here for others to take down: -

Ex. Juno – Jealousy, Baronne, Hebe, Queen Dido, and Violet.
Ex. Guinevere – Bourbon, Bijou, and Fino V.
Ex. Pallas – Pallas II.
His Jupiter is likewise well known, and is the father of Franco, Frou-frou, and Diana, ex. Vesta.
Nemours, Fleur de France, and Childeric, ex Vivien, whilst Ramee, imp by Wildfowler, and afterwards owned by Mr H. Wyndham-Carter, has got Ramee Cadet ex Pasqueret; Ramee II, Hebe II, Nichette and Niniche, ex Hebe. Royalty, Saphir, Bergere, and Brunette, ex Finette II.
Finette II being one of the last pups I bred before leaving for Australia by Ulfius, ex Kathleen.

I cannot here pass by without saying how grieved all Basset men were when they heard of the villains who laid the poisoned bait, opium, it is believed, in poor doggy's way. The last period I now dwell on with nearly as great importance as I did on its immediate predecessor.

Mr Krehl had found out, just as I had done, that in breeding may be carried out to a certain point, but when then reached, degeneracy immediately sets in.

There is a loss of bone, leather, physique, and size, and Mr Krehl counteracted this evil in the Couteulx Bassets with the importation of the Lane strain. It was the only thing wanted to give perfect touch to his work.

These hounds, with their long, sweeping ears, grand jowl, and great bone, have saved the necessity of a continual in breeding policy.

These Lane hounds are Blanchette and Oriflamme.

He has produced Lynette from Blanchette by Ramee, Carillon from the same bitch by his champion, Fino de Paris, and Gwendolene from the same mating.

These hounds alone show what value the Lane-Couteulx hounds have, and the genius Mr Krehl has shown in bringing them forward.

Not the least of all Mr Krehl's achievements has been the formation, with Mr H. Wyndham-Carter, of the Basset Hound Club, with Comte Couteulx as its honoured president.

This brings me down to 1884, when I found myself at home again.

I had hardly expected my old Model was alive, but I found he was, and what was more, in good health too. I sent for him when I came to live in Yorkshire, and he arrived, fat and heavy with years, but he gave me a welcome which only four-footed friends can give their masters ; and yet people say dogs forget their friends.

A few weeks brought him into good sound condition again, and I was soon on the look out for a mate for him, for Garenne has gone, and to begin what I had once done before, namely the formation of a kennel.

I soon found a bitch in the person of Finette II, his great granddaughter, and I put her to him. This was in breeding with a vengeance; but I could not help it. She was the only bitch I could procure, and the dog was very old.

Time waits for no man, and it is not very likely to do so for a hound in his thirteenth year.

The result has been perfectly satisfactory, and I have now three beautiful pups from this intercourse – namely, Kini, Lady Dollie, and Lady Daisy, all true Bassets and tricolours.

And now I come to what I may truly call disappointment.

Through Captain Ramsay's kindness, I got that typical Lane bitch Blanchette to my kennels. He generously offered me half of a litter if I succeeded raising one from her by Model.

I regret infinitely that after the trouble of seven months, I was only rewarded with the birth of dead pups.

But I hope again, through Mr Ramsay's kindness, to breed out of her as good as what Mr Krehl has with Fino de Paris as sire.

This, now, is what I have to begin with again, and I should not be speaking the truth if I said that I was altogether disappointed.

And now one last word to the club. Let us put, all, our shoulders to the wheel as some of us have done. Let us pull together in unanimity, and offer to one another the uses of our hounds' services on easy terms, as I will my old Model's freely whilst they last.

Let us keep the grand breed from falling into the hands of those that will use them for the purposes of lucre, and save our Bassets from these pests, who trade on the tyros who would enter the Fancy.This alone would keep our special classes up to a high average. The man who breeds for the sole purpose of sale will not breed such hounds as they who breed for the love of the dog.

If we all do this, I am sure we will succeed, and produce what must at once be the envy of all beholders, and, as I have called them before, the chef d'oeuvre of any exhibition.

And to the club itself, and to pack which they have formed, let me give them a few words of advice, as I believe I am the only one who has hunted the Basset as a pack.

Do not be too sanguine at first, or imagine that you are going to see the hound hunt as you have seen other breeds do.

It is useless to bring a lot of hounds together strangers one another, and imagine that they will settle down on the trail straight away. They will not.

Either let us all hunt them on hare or on a drag, but state what be, then kennel them together that drag for a day or so in advance, and then lead them out to run.

Bassets are wilful, perverse, headstrong hounds, that will have their own way, and especially in their hunting. Yelling at them, and whip will only cow them, and not make them run.

Let them go their own fashion, and you will see them run, and hear their bell-like notes to your heart's content.

People who do not understand them will never hunt them at all. They must be first understood.

What is worth doing at all is worth doing well. ***En avant***.

Millais's reasons for the beagle outcross seem to vary from time to time. In the article just quoted, he puts it down to his youthful lack of knowledge. But, on another occasion he said of the beagle outcross:

> At that time, I was unaware that Lord Onslow has Bassets. Had I known this I would have asked his permission to breed the dog to one of his bitches. But as I did not know this, and could not then procure a bitch, I began breeding through a Beagle . . .

Millais' view of the basset and how it should be bred can best be judged by what he later wrote about his views of the origins of the basset:

> The only logical conclusion one can come to as to the origin of these hounds is that as man took up the chase of the smaller game, a slow hound was required – a type of hound which could at once be produced by breeding only from those that were short in the leg, and consequently slower in speed. Breeding from such hounds, it must be observed, would but tend to decrease the height and not the bodily proportions, coat, or form of the head. In due time as weapons made their appearance – and by weapons I especially mean when guns came into use – a slower dog still was required, which would either hunt in front of the sportsman or drive game slowly towards him. This type of hound would be produced by again breeding from the lowest and heaviest of his predecessors and, what with the weight in front and the question of stability, the internal ligaments of the carpus would give way, the forefeet would turn out so as to act as buttresses to the chest wall, and in the animal thus produced we should find a hound of full-size body and of similar head and colour to the hounds from which it sprang; identical in fact, with them except in this peculiar formation of the front and hind feet. If the legs were straight the chest would hang between them and the whole weight of the body would necessarily be centred at the shoulder joint. Consequently the animal would be incapable of any active movement and much exposed to dislocation of the shoulder joint; but as the legs incline inwards and then outwards, the weight of the body is supported below the chest, viz. at the carpus, the latter being as it were, the keystone on which the entire weight of the body falls. As a result we should expect to find trouble if any other portion of the architecture was out of position.

These views, coming from such an eminent man, coloured the thinking of people in the basset world even into the 1960s, especially the idea that the pure basset was developed primarily for slow working.

Unfortunately, Millais was advised to go abroad in 1880 for health reasons and had to disperse his kennels, including Model. After spending time in Australia, New Zealand and the United States, Millais returned to London in 1884. He regained Model and used him as a stallion until he died at the age of fifteen. In the year Millais returned, he and others established the BHC. At that time, support for the Club came both from breeders interested in showing and those interested in hunting. About the same time, Millais also acquired some the bassets sold by Lord Onslow when he closed his kennels.

The breed prospered in numbers, but the quality rapidly deteriorated. The same was also happening in France. In 1892 Millais decided to take drastic action. He felt that no improvement could be made by importing from France as the breed there was not of good quality. He knew of no other suitable blood in England. He was of the opinion that the breed was not stable because it was not 'pure', having been formed in France by outcrosses with other breeds. He was convinced that one of the outcross breeds must have been a bigger and heavier breed. So Millais chose the Bloodhound. To some extent, his choice was influenced by the concentration in England on the shape and character of the head. Also some breeders were convinced that the basset and the Bloodhound were related , both being derived from the St Hubert hound. Millais knew that such a cross was feasible as a friend, Mr Marsden of Leeds, had made a successful cross a few years before. Millais later said:

> I chose the Bloodhound, firstly because the head of the Basset should resemble that of the Bloodhound, and secondly because of my experimental work with Beagles I knew that the persistence of a return to Basset formation in legs was but a matter of one or two generations. There, therefore, remained simply the question of colour and this I was certain would come back very speedily.

It should be noted that some of his primary concerns appear to have been show characteristics of head and colour.

Initially, Millais only had one basset available to him, Nicholas, a highly inbred tricolour of reasonably good construction, although with a poor head. He used a Bloodhound, Inoculation. The mating was by artificial insemination and the birth by caesarean, both the first recorded instances of use with higher mammalia. However, the bitch and many of the twelve puppies did not survive. They were of basset type, but took the dark colour of the Bloodhound.

Millais then conducted some in-breeding with the results of the outcross. Dulcie, from Rickey by Forester, was put to Bowman, who was by Forester out of Psyche II. The results were very successful producing well boned, basset like puppies in tricolour, lemon and white and black and tan. Apart from the colours, the main result was a heavier hound. It was this type that eventually became the Basset Hound of today.

His influence can be judged by the Kennel Club Stud Book which attributes twenty-two hounds to his breeding. The Stud Book compiled by *The Kennel Review* between 1883 and 1884 lists seven hounds owned by him (Model, Kiwi, Garenne, Isabel, Kathleen, Lady Dollie and Lady Daisie). Of the sixty-four bassets listed with a known pedigree, fourteen had one or both parents bred by him, fifteen had one or more grand parents bred by him and thirteen had one or more great grand parents bred by him. He continued breeding, showing and judging into the 1890s.

Monsieur Léon Verrier (1874)

Leon Verrier lived in Mont Saint-Aignan, near Rouen, France. Verrier started his kennels in 1874 with Couteulx bassets, but became more interested in the Lane type.

Monsieur Léon Verrier and his bassets at the Montdiddier Dog Show in 1903.

He won a number of championships. Verrier produced a type acceptable to both the adherents of Couteulx and Lane types of basset by combining the qualities of them both. His friend, Monsieur Leiseigneur, built up a pack of Verrier hounds and hunted rabbit and hare, accounting for about 1,200 each season. Monsieur Pinel developed the Verrier hound to one which was 32 cm high and 80 cm long, with a beagle like head. Monsieur Albert Mallart, of Barly fame, also chose the Verrier type when he switched to bassets after WWI. In 1922 the Club du Basset d'Artois decided to call them Basset d'Artois, Verrier type. They were noted for their length, coat, and very long and curling ears. Mimard and Blachon on page 50 of their 1907 book described them thus:

> These hounds, which have kept the lean head and the lovely coat of the Lane Basset, are great hunters, and hunt all types of quarry, although they can easily specialise. They are able to change, not for example, from hare to hare, but from hare to roe deer, or from roe deer to stag. In spite of their smooth coat, they are remarkable in thickets. They are, all in all, very good hounds, and if one adds to them, in that, they are highly attractive, there is no other breed so very agreeable for those hunting with a gun as they will bring pleasure to serious sport.

It was this type that formed the basis of the modern Basset Artésien-Normand.

Verrier believed that the basset was a throwback to the St Hubert Hound by way of the French 'Chien d'ordre', large hunting hounds. He thought that bassets appeared in litters, were selected and inbred for their low character. He suggested that these were originally bred in the sixteenth Century. His authority reinforced the line breeding policy adopted in England in the early twentieth Century.

In the early 1920s Godfrey Heseltine contacted Leon Verrier and had lengthy correspondence. During this correspondence, Heseltine sent some photographs of the Walhampton to Verrier. In reply, Leon commented that : *'they were too big. the ears too rounded at the tips; i.e.. not sufficiently pointed at the tips!'* He also said that '*they have magnificent limbs, perfect stance of legs and feet, and heads typical of the bloodhound.'* He thought that the English hounds seemed to revert back to their long-legged ancestors, les chiens de chasse, by having long-legged puppies. He seemed to be unaware of the Bloodhound influence of Millais. In 1921 Godfrey Heseltine purchased one hound from Verrier, Pampeute (sometimes spelt Pampente). But Pampeute appears to have only had one litter. Verrier also put Godfrey Heseltine in touch with Monsieur Mallart from whom he imported Meteor.

Verrier's book of 1921 also heavily influenced thinking for many years on bassets in both France and England.

George R. Krehl (1878)

George Krehl lived in Hanover Square, London. He was the editor of *The Stock-Keeper* and later collaborated with Everett Millais in publishing *The Fancier's Gazette.* Before he had bassets he had Irish Terriers and Collies. He had been instrumental in starting the Irish Terrier Club and wrote the first Standard for the Basset Hound. This Standard stated: '*the head of the Basset to be ideal should closely resemble that of the Bloodhound'.* Mr Krehl was a founder member of the BHC in 1884 and was one of the first judges they appointed.

His first encounter with bassets was at Crystal Palace in 1878 where he met Lord Onslow. In 1880 he read a report in *The Field* of the Brussels exhibition at which the Comte de Couteulx's tricolour basset Fino de Paris (11060) had been exhibited. He went to Paris to report for *The Live Stock Journal* and met the Comte le Couteulx. In association with Louis Clement and after an introduction to Monsieur St. Hilaire, they

George Krehl's Fino, Pallas and Jupiter.

managed to acquire this stallion hound from the Jardin d'Acclimatation in Paris where he was at stud. This hound went on to produce many champion and winning hounds in the UK and heavily influenced the breeding of hounds in the UK for many decades. He was probably the largest importer of bassets in that century, many from the Comte le Couteulx.

One result of this visit was that George Krehl re-built his kennels along the lines of those at the Jardin d'Acclimatation. An article in *The Kennel Review* of 1883 gives some idea of them:

> Built against a wall, shed form, roof slightly sloping, the whole kennel opens with four doors, a hole cut in each door before which in winter a piece of matting hangs. -Inside, ordinary sleeping benches. Jumping steps on door, by which the dogs hop up top and lie there in the sun, or in cold weather on the wood, instead of cold ground. Some steps fixed to sides of the wall, which the dogs use to lie on, but their peculiar value is for exercise, as the dogs (small and large) are running up and down all day; so by this contrivance adds to the day's amusement, induces them to take exercise, and makes an ordinary kennel four times over its real size. As his neighbours have to be studied, the large kennel is only used as a playground, and other accommodation provided for the night.

Mr Krehl employed two men to exercise his dogs in Hyde Park and, periodically, sent them down to the country for an outing.

Fino de Paris was much admired in England. So he decided to import some more of the Couteulx stock thinking that they would be similar: heavy, low, full crook, harsh coated and tricolour. Guinevere (12138), known as Gibolette in France, Theo (15703) and Vivien (13340) were direct descendents. Jupiter (12153), known as Bosquet in France, and Pallas (11070) were also imported. However, Guinevere turned out to be a bicolour hound; Theo and Vivien turned out to be different in form; and Pallas was black, white and tan and smooth coated. Only Jupiter was tricolour. The different form became known as the 'Termino' type: lighter build, half crooked, plainer heads, short and fine coats and light coloured. They may have been the result of an experimental outcross with a beagle made by the Comte and his cousin, de Chaumont. As a consequence, George Krehl concentrated on breeding the heavier 'Fino de Paris' type.

In 1882, George Krehl imported two more hounds from France, this time from the kennels of Louis Lane. Lane's hounds were much in favour in France as they were considered to be more pure bred than those of the Comte le Couteulx. They were Blanchette (72147) and Oriflamme (15702). Whilst these were lighter in build and more uniformly coloured than those of the Comte le Couteulx, they had a tendency to knuckle over and were pale in colour. As a consequence, they were not favoured in the UK by either the hunting or the showing interests.

In 1883 Krehl bred a tricolour hound, Nemours (146068) which he sold to Mr W. Chamberlain of 99 Madison Avenue, New York. This hound then went to Mr Lawrence Timson of Red Bank, New Jersey, Maizeland kennels. He was the first basset to be shown in an American dog show, at the Westminster Kennel Club show, and became a Champion.

In 1884 George Krehl purchased some of Lord Onslow's hounds when the Earl was disposing of his kennel. In the same year, George Krehl was one of the founder members of the Basset Hound Club. To get Royal approval of the new Club, he made a present to the Prince of Wales of two bassets. In the previous December, George Krehl had taken three-and-a-half couple of his hounds to the first Meet of the Club as it was being formed.

An idea of Krehl's influence can be gained from the fact that the Kennel Club Stud Books list fourteen hounds which he imported and twelve which he had bred, all between 1880 and 1885. Reinforcing this is the Stud Book in *The Kennel Review,* published between 1883 and 1884, which shows eighteen bassets owned by him and numerous others which had his blood-lines.

Louis Clement (c. 1880)

Louis Clement was a well known author and magazine contributor writing under the name of 'Wildfowler'. Mainly in association with George Krehl and because he travelled extensively in Europe reporting on dog shows, he was responsible for importing a number of hounds from France in the early 1880s, notably Fino de Paris (11060), Jupiter (12153) (known as Bosquet in France), Guinevere (12138) (called Gilbellote in France), Pallas (11070), Théo (15703), Vivien (13340) and Ramee. These hounds had profound effects on the development of bassets, both for hunting and for showing.

It was possibly Louis Clement who perpetuated the use of the word 'basset' to describe all the various types, both rough and smooth, as he once wrote of the basset that: *'Any hound which stands lower than 16 inches (no matter his 'provincial breed') is called in France and in Belgium a Basset.'.*

H. Wyndham-Carter (1880)

Mr H. Wyndham-Carter lived and had his kennels at Kennington, near Ashford in Kent. He obtained his first bassets in 1880, some from Lord Onslow's kennels and some from France (both Couteulx and Lane types), probably via his good friend and rival, George Krehl. His first significant breeding was in 1882, Ramee II. He was successful in the show ring throughout the 1880s and his bloodlines went into some of the early hunts. He helped form the BHC and in 1883 held the first meet of the BHC at his home in Kent. He was the first Secretary of the BHC, formed in 1884.

Both he and George Krehl were opponents of the Kennel Club and were instrumental in forming a rival organisation, the National Kennel Club. In 1883 he started *The Kennel Review*, a quarterly newspaper, of which he was Editor. This carried articles by leading breeders, including Everett Millais and Arthur Croxton-Smith, reports and results of Shows and letters, several of them attacking the policy of the Kennel Club and, in particular, its Secretary. The Review also published a Basset Hound Stud Book as it considered the Kennel Club Stud Book to be inaccurate.

Mrs C.C. Ellis (1886)

Mrs Ellis lived at Shottesbrook Park, Maidenhead, Berkshire; then at Brettenham Park, Bildeston, Suffolk; then at White Lodge, Colchester. She purchased her first basset at the Warwick Show in 1886: Venus II (23809), a tricolour hound bred by T. Pick in 1885, by Champion Jupiter (12152) out of Venus. Venus was a daughter of Fino de Paris (11060), one of the best and most influential of the imports from France. Venus II was eventually exported to Australia. Venus II appears to have been purchased originally by Mr F.P. Ellis of Thorley Bourne, Bishop Stortford and of Fitzroy Road, NW London. This Mr Ellis was also an owner and breeder of bassets, including an influential tricolour hound, Citron. He may have been a relative of Mrs Ellis.

Mrs Ellis went on to be one of the leading breeders of both smooth and rough haired bassets. Some of the latter were acquired from Mrs Ellis by the Prince of Wales. She was one of the advocates of the show hound, in contrast to those used for hunting. She was Secretary of the BHC during the First World War.

In the 1890s six of her dog hounds were used fairly extensively by the Hunts. They sired sixteen registered hounds in nine litters for the Cookridge. Dale Park, Delapre, Mr Kenyon Fuller's, Sandringham, Walhampton and Wheatley Park.

Arthur Croxton-Smith (1889)

Arthur Croxton-Smith lived and had his kennels at Burlington House, Wandle Road, Upper Tooting, London. Before going in for bassets, he had Bloodhounds and Bulldogs. Everett Millais gave him his first basset, Witch, in the late 1880s. From this bitch, he produced three Champions: Welbeck (332D), Wantage (99D) and Wensum (425E). He also bred Champion Waverer (744K), a descendent of Millais's experiments with Bloodhound crossing. This hound had a profound influence on the breed. He produced many other hounds for both show and hunting enthusiasts. There are at least thirteen of his hounds in the Kennel Club Stud Books. Between 1900 and 1911, the MBHA Stud Books list 57 registered hounds with one or both parents bred by Arthur Croxton-Smith. The packs involved (number of registered hounds parented in brackets) were: Chiddingstone (6), Dallam Tower (8), Greywell Hill (7), Sandringham (8), Slane (8), Stainrigg (2), Walhampton (15), Wroxton (2) and North Lancashire (1). It was much because of the influence of his stock that he was able to comment after the 1914 MBHA Show at Banbury: *'the very leggy hounds have practically disappeared.'*

Chapter XV of his 1909 book was devoted to the Basset Hound. In this he gives a detailed description of the basset hound as he saw it:

> The type favoured in this country has a head as much like that of a Bloodhound as we can breed it. The ears are long, and hang in graceful folds; the head, peaked at the occiput, is long and narrow, without a stoop below the eyes, and the forehead is of great depth through the flews. There should be an ample dewlap, and the skin across the forehead and down the side of the head should be wrinkled. The front legs, which are only about 4 inches in length, may be either crooked or straight, but in any case they should be heavily boned, and set on well under the body. Elbows or joints that knuckle over are a great disfigurement, obviously unfitting the animal longed exertion. The chest is deep let

Arthur Croxton-Smith's kennels at Wandsworth, London with Bloodhounds, Bulldog and Bassets, circa 1903.

> down; the hind quarters should be long and the stifles should he well bent. The fact that the hind legs are longer than those in front give the Basset a peculiar gait, which is thoroughly distinctive. The stern is carried hound fashion, and is well feathered underneath. The coat of the smooth variety is short and fine, handling well, with skin loose and elastic. The markings are usually black, white, and tan, the head preferably of a rich tan with black; sometimes they are beautifully flecked, and when you get a sorty pack together, you cannot wish for a prettier sight.

This book was widely read and, no doubt, coloured the thinking on bassets of many Masters,especially as, since then, only two other books have been published in England dealing with the basset in any detail as a hunting hound.

His love of bassets was inherited by his niece, Mrs Phyllis Salisbury, and then by her daughter, his great niece, the late Mrs Audrey Parlby and her Huckworthy pack.

Mrs Mabel Tottie (1892)

Mrs Mabel Tottie lived at Conniston Hall, near Hellifield, Yorkshire. She was one of the leading Show breeders in the last decade of the nineteenth Century. Her interest in bassets began around 1892. Her bitches were extensively used by the Walhampton between 1897 and 1902 and by the Delapré in 1897–1898.

She also bred Basset Griffon Vendéen, having purchased her first at Cruft's in 1892. Mrs Tottie experimented with crossbreeding of the 'rough-coats' with the 'smooths,' but this concept was short-lived. Some crossbreds (Basset Griffon Vendéen x Basset Hounds) were used by the Walhampton Pack, but since they had a completely different manner of hunting, more like terriers, they had to be drafted out or they would have spoilt the pack.

Mrs Tottie experimented again. In 1898 she bred one of Capt. Owen Swaffield's bitches, Bella, a crossbred Basset x Bloodhound offspring, to Mrs Ellis's basset, Napoleon II, and produced Belladona. This bitch was later owned by the Walhampton. The Walhampton had previously used offspring from Millais's Basset x Bloodhound crosses.

At Cruft's in 1900 Mrs Tottie purchased Arthur Croxton-Smith's prize winning basset, Wantage for the huge sum of £150. It was Mrs Tottie who produced the 1930 breed Standard for the Basset Hound Club by updating the original standard written by Sir Everett Millais.

Mrs Mabel Tottie's rough coated basset Puritan.

Messieurs Albert et Auguste Mallart (1918)

Monsieur Albert Mallart lived in Barly, near Dullens, in the Somme, France and had a kennel of bassets with the suffix de Barly. He started with Briquets d'Artois before 1914 and switched to Verrier type bassets in 1918. He quickly became the leading breeder of Basset Artésien-Normand. In 1921 following correspondence between Godfrey Heseltine and Leon Verrier, the Walhampton imported a hound from Monsieur Albert Mallart, Meteor'21. Meteor was used extensively by the Walhampton as a stallion, siring 7 litters of 20 hounds registered with the MBHA between 1923 and 1925. Monsieur Albert Mallart also exported several basset to America.Sir John Buchanan-Jardine was so struck with them that, in about 1925, he purchased and imported a couple and hunted them with his pack of foot harriers. In his book of 1937, Sir John described them thus: *'They were very imposing -looking indeed with big, heavy, bloodhound heads, extremely long low-set ears and thin, fine sterns.'* But they proved to be too slow for his 22in pack.

Tragically, Albert died in 1932. His son, Auguste, took on his father's kennels and continued breeding the bassets.

Possibly as a result of knowing about the Walhampton history and having read Sir John Buchanan-Jardine's book, Miss Keevil of the Grims visited Monsieur Auguste Mallart in 1948 where she purchased Ulema'48 de Barly. May be he introduced her to Monsieur Paul Leduc of Blendecques in the Pas de Calais, from whom she purchased Cornemuse'48 de Blendecques. Both these hounds were Basset Artésien-Normand, a breed that had become almost extinct during the war. These two hounds, especially Ulema, were major influences in the re-establishment and development of the post war Basset Hound in England, both for hunting and showing. Their hunting progeny formed the foundations of the Grims, the Fourshires, the Leadon Vale, the Huckworthy and the Albany.

Mrs Nina E. Elms (1928)

Mrs Elms lived at Fyfield Grange, Andover, Hampshire and established the Reynalton kennels in the 1920s with Bloodhounds and Beagles. In 1928 she purchased two bassets from Miss Ena Adams who had the Brancaster Bassets and also had beagles. In 1933 Mrs Elms purchased several Walhampton hounds when they were sold at auction. Amongst these were Walhampton Lynnewood'29 and Walhampton Nightshade'31, both of which were Show Champions as well as hunting hounds. In 1936 she sold the basset Reynalton Dulcimara'36 to Miss Keevil. Thus began a relationship which was to radically develop the Basset Hound.

During WWII, Mrs Elms, Mrs Groom and Miss Keevil managed to continue breeding bassets, albeit on a limited scale. Immediately after the war, Mrs Elms and Miss Keevil embarked on a breeding plan to improve the Basset Hound. Lynnewood had been put to Nightshade with a litter of five, of which four became Champions. One of these was a dog hound, Orpheus of Reynalton. He was put to the Bloodhound bitch, Sheba of Reynalton. One of the cross bred bitches in the litter was Suzanne of Reynalton and she was put to a Basset Hound, Majesty. One of the litter, Symbol, was put to Grims Worship'40. The latter was by Westerby Marquis'38 out of Wick Welcome'35, both of which hunting hounds Miss Keevil had during the war. One dog from this litter, Grims Sermon'47 went on to sire hounds which established the improved Grims Basset Hounds of the post war years.

Bibliography

Alderton, D. 2000. *Hounds of the World*. Shrewsbury: Swan Hill Press.

Appleton, D.H. 1960. *The Basset Hound Handbook*. London: Nicholson & Watson.

Basset Hound Club The. 1989–2001. *The Basset Hound Club & Albany Newsletters*. England: The Basset Hound Club.

Bemis, W.E. 1984. Pseudomorposis and the evolution of Dipmoi. *Paleobiology 10, 293–307.*

Booth, R.E. 2002. *The Official Book of the Basset Hound*. Neptune City, NJ: T.F.H. Publications.

Brusewitz, G. 1967. (Trans. Wheeler, W. 1969). *Hunting*. Sweden: Esselte.

Bryden, H.A. 1903. *Hare Hunting and Harriers*. London: Grant Richards.

Bryden, H.A. 1912. *Hunting in France*. In Suffolk & Berkshire, (The Earl of). (Ed.). 1912. *Encyclopaedia of Sport & Games*. London: Heinemann. Volume III. Pp. 64–71.

Bryden, H.A. 1927. *Horn and Hound*. London: Methuen.

Buchanan-Jardine, J. (Sir). 1937. *Hounds of the World*. London: Methuen.

Bury, J.P.Y. 2003. *France 1814–1940*. London: Routledge.

Cameron, L.C.R. 1912. *The Basset Hound*. In Suffolk & Berkshire, (The Earl of). (Ed.). 1912. *Encyclopaedia of Sport & Games*. London: Heinemann. Volume III. P. 35.

Clutton-Brock, J. 1992. The process of domestication. *Mammal Review, 22, 79–85.*

Coppinger R.P. & Smith, C.K. 1988. A model for understanding the evolution of mammalian behaviour. In Genoways, H. (Ed.). *Current Mammalogy, Vol. 2* Plenum, NY. Pp. 33–74.

Daglish, E.F. 1975. *The Basset Hound*. London: W & G Foyle.

Dicker, R. 2004. Private papers.

Fouilloux, J du. 1573. *La Vénerie*. Paris: Galiuot du Pré. Facsimile. 1979. Paris, Roger Dacosta.

Francomano, C.A. 2001. *Achondroplasia*. Gene Reviews. Seattle: University of Washington.

Geiger, G. 1972. Prufungswesen und Leistungsvererbung beim Deutschen Darhthaaringen Vorstehhund. *Giessner Beitrage zur Erbpathologie und Zuchthygiene,* 4, 40–3.

Gilbey, W. (Sir). (rev. Scott C.M.F.). 1979. *Hounds in Old Days*. Hindhead: Spur.

Hemer, H. 1990. *The Decline of Environmental Appreciation*. Cambridge: Cambridge University Press.

Hounds. Vols. I-XX. 1983–2004. Shrewsbury: Ravensworld.

Johnston, G. 1968. *The Basset Hound*. London: Popular Dogs.

Johnston, G. & Ericson, M. 1979. *Hounds of France*. Hindhead: Saiga Publishing.

Jubb, K.V.F.; Kennedy, P.C. & Palmer, N. (Eds.). 1993. *Pathology of Domestic Animals, (4th Edition)*. London: Academic Press.

Keevil, Miss M.M. 1997. Private papers.

Kennel Club, The. 1873–1915. *Stud Book*. London: The Kennel Club.

Kennel Club, The. *2000. Year Book. 1999/2000*. London: The Kennel Club.

Kennel Review, The. Vols. II & III, July 1883-February 1885. London.

Kirkness, E.F., Venter, C., et al. 2003. *The dog genome: survey sequencing and comparative analysis*. Science, 301, 1898–1903

Kruska, D. 1988. Mammalian domestication and its effect on brain structure and behaviour. In Jerison, H.J. & Jerison, I. *Intelligence and Evolutionary Biology*. Berlin: Springer-Verlag, Pp. 211–250.

Leblanc, E. & Miller, J.A. 1987. *Les Bassets Courants*. Paris: Gerfaut Club.

Leblanc, M. 1995. *Le Basset Artésien-Normand*. Paris: Editions de Vecchi.

Linette, M. & Le Gall, A. (Eds.). 2000. *Chiens de France* Paris: Editions Crépin-Leblond.

Lloyd, J.I. 1973. *Hounds of Britain*. London: A. & C. Black.

Longrigg, R. 1975. *The History of Foxhunting*. London: Macmillan.

Lynch, D. 2004. *The Genetic History of Purebred Dogs.* Proceedings of the Annual Meeting of the American Association for the Advancement of Science, MPE Symposia, February 13.
Macdonnogh, K. 1999. *Reigning Cats and Dogs.* London: Fourth Estate.
Masters of Basset Hounds Association. 1925–2004. *Stud Book, Volumes I to XXII.* England:
Millais, E (Sir). 1895. *Two Problems of Reproduction.* Manchester: Our Dogs.
Morrison, E. 1954. *Fox and Hare in Leicestershire.* London: Eyre & Spottiswoode.
Nixon, M.R. 1999. *The Basset Hound.* Waterlooville: Kingdom Books.
OMIM report. 2003. John Hopkins University
Onslow Estate Letter Books & Accounts. 1877–1891. Woking: Surrey History Centre (Ref: 1320/169/3/1–144)
Orioli I.M.; Castilla E.E.; Barbosa-Neto J.G. 1986. *The birth prevalence rates for the skeletal dysplasias.* J. Med Genet 1986 Aug; 23(4): pp. 328–332
Ostrander, E.A. & Krugzyakl. 2004. *Unleashing the Canine Genome.* Science, September 2004, Pp. 1271–1274
Paget, J.O. 1900.*Hunting.* London: Hadden Hall Library.
Parlby, Mrs A. 2004. Private papers.
Rawle, Mrs M. 2003. Private papers.
Samat, J-B. 1907 *Les Chiens, le Gibier et ses Ennemis.* Saint Étienne: Mimard et Blachon.
Scharnberg, J.F. 1973. *Beagling and Basseting.* Richmond, Va: The Old Dominion Press.
Scharnberg, J.F. (Ed.). 2003. *2003 National Beagle Club Stud Book.* Virginia: National Beagle Club of America.
Serpell, J. (Ed.). 1995. *The Domestic Dog: its evolution, behaviour and interactions with people.* Cambridge: University Press.
Smith, A.C. 1909. *Everyman's Book of the Dog.* London: Hodder and Stoughton.
Smith, A.C. 1932. *Hounds & Dogs.* London: Seeley, Service & Co.
Smith, A.C. 1938. *Sporting Dogs.* London: Country Life.
Société Centrale Canine. 2000. *Chiens de France.* Paris: Editions Crépins-Leblond.
Société de Vénerie. 2003. *Standards des Cheins Courants.* Saint-Brieue: Imprimerie Jacq.
Verro, P. 1994. *La Vénerie à Pied.* Paris: Edition du Gefaut.
Vezins, ‹. (Comte de). 1882. (Trans. Woolner, L.R. 1974.) *Hounds for a Pack.* London: J.A. Allen.
Williams, J. 2004. Private papers.
Wimhurst, C.G.E. 1964. *The Book of the Hound.* London: Frederick Muller.

Index